Lessons for an Urban Goddess

LANEY ZUKERMAN

Published by Elaine (Laney) Zukerman
New York, NY

laneyzukerman.com

Paperback ISBN: 978-0692454220

First Printing: May, 2015

Cover and interior design by truenorthpublish.com

Lessons for an Urban Goddess is also available as an e-book

Table of Contents

Preface
Introduction

SECTION ONE: WHAT AN URBAN GODDESS KNOWS

1 The Urban Goddess is Confident 17

2 The Urban Goddess Emotional Beauty Toolbox 23

3 The Urban Goddess Is a Peaceful Warrior 35

4 The Urban Goddess Is Sensual 41

5 The Urban Goddess and the Inner Goddess Muse 49

6 The Urban Goddess and the Inner Bitch 53

SECTION TWO: THE URBAN GODDESS LESSON ON LIFE'S TWISTS AND TURNS

7 The Urban Goddess Is Smart with Her Heart 59

8 The Urban Goddess on Loss, Courage and Uncertainty 65

SECTION THREE: THE URBAN GODDESS LESSONS ON HEROES AND HEARTBREAKERS

9 The Urban Goddess and the Hero 73

10 The Urban Goddess Knows a Hero When She Sees One 79

11 The Urban Goddess Values Good Communication 81

12 The Urban Goddess on Sincerity 83

13 The Urban Goddess and the Heartbreaker 87

14 The Urban Goddess Knows Men are Transparent 93

15 The Urban Goddess on Relationship Games 95

16 The Urban Goddess and the Narcissist 97

17 The Urban Goddess and the Sociopath 101

18 The Urban Goddess and the Player 105

19 The Urban Goddess on Ambivalence 109

20 The Urban Goddess Avoids Destructive Relationships 111

21 The Urban Goddess Knows a Hero from a Heartbreaker 115

22 The Urban Goddess New Old-Fashioned Rules for Dating 119

SECTION FOUR: URBAN GODDESS REFLECTIONS AND TAKEAWAYS

23 The Urban Goddess Understands Inner Bliss 127

24 Ways the Urban Goddess Improves Her Relationships 129

25 The Urban Goddess Surrenders and Celebrates Her Fabulousness 131

26 Urban Goddess Final Thoughts 135

Inspirational Quotes 139
Recommended Readings 141
About the Author 145

Preface

A Goddess: "A female god, divinity or deity. A woman of superior charms and / or excellence. A woman who is adored, especially for her beauty, grace and appeal. A woman whose beauty inspires great affinity. A Hollywood starlet."
~ The Urban Dictionary

Lessons for an Urban Goddess is a no-nonsense, practical guide that will:

- Help you unleash your fabulous self.

- Help you create a self that is authentic, confident, serene, feisty and REAL!

- Encourage, inspire, challenge and explore all the workings of you.

- Guide you to be the best you can be today, tomorrow and ALWAYS!

- Help you develop a compass of ageless wisdom.

- Empower you with the know-how to release your burning desire for something more, ignite your inner bitch (your dark side) and accept all the parts of you.

∽ Encourage you to think like a beautiful, feminine, sensual goddess.

∽ Help you get smart with your heart in relationships.

∽ Teach you to surrender your fears and anxieties to a higher power and bask in the mindful, blissful authentic moments of now.

Acknowledgements

Writing this book has been a personal defining moment in my life. At times it was a challenge. There are a number of people who supported me during this time (and always!). It is with great respect and gratitude that I acknowledge you.

My beautiful daughters, Jaclyn and Laura. Thank you for always being there for me and offering your suggestions and advice. I love you!

To my sister Lucille and my wonderful extended family; the Petricciones, the Reiss and Mackey clans, the Zukermans and my dearest friends (you know who you all are, you matter and I am so blessed to have you in my life!).

A special thank you to my amazing editor, Diane Krause. You understood my vision and helped this dream become a reality.

To my graphic artist and designer Brian Del Turco. Thank you for your amazing creativity and patience in the cover design and format.

Thank you to my photographer Joe Jenkins. You helped to make the photo shoot run smoothly and effortlessly.

To my parents, Joan and Frank. You are forever in our hearts. You taught me well.

To the hundreds of clients I have worked with over the years, I am humbled and grateful to have had the privilege of working with you.

Thank you to Michael Zukerman, for being a supportive friend, mentor and awesome dad to our girls.

Michael, HB. Thank you for the motivation, encouragement and inspiration.

Introduction

"Do not let the noise of others' opinions drown out your own inner voice." ~ Steve Jobs

Lessons for an Urban Goddess is a no-nonsense, practical guidebook that shares ageless wisdom. As a professional coach and counselor, I have seen firsthand how many of my clients have improved their lives by using many of these lessons of encouragement, inspiration, empowerment and smart-heart common sense. I believe that this book can help you tap into your amazing inner goddess by getting clear about who you are, what you want and where you are headed.

I'm here to tell you that you can be goddess-like and have bliss in your life if you want to. It doesn't make you a snob or narcissistic. It just makes you feel like you matter. Your unique personal style and personality are a gift. With some introspection you can be excited and passionate as well as peaceful and blissful. It will take changing some of your thoughts and behaviors. It will take time and patience. If you choose bliss and you keep it realistic, the rewards will be plentiful.

It is important to listen to the subtle, and sometimes not-so-subtle, goddess lessons that speak to you through your intuition and life experiences. They will help guide you on your journey and place you where you need to be!

Lessons for an Urban Goddess is my no-nonsense guidebook to making deeper sense of your world. It's a cup of wisdom offered from a goddess point of view.

Read along as I help you organize your thoughts, decisions, dreams and desires in more simplistic, effortless and positive ways that will help you:

ॐ Build your sense of self.

ॐ Embrace your inner goddess sensuality.

ॐ Become smarter with your heart, body and soul.

If you are going to live, why not live more blissfully and bask in the joy of living like a goddess in a modern day world!

The book is divided into four sections.

Section One covers a goddess's emotional beauty toolbox. Here I will help you incorporate inspiration, deeper meaning and joy into your life. This comes by strengthening your sense of self through self-love and adopting the belief that you matter. I want you to stop doubting your perceptions and learn to embrace both the light and dark sides of you.

Section Two is focused on ways the goddess deals with life's twists, turns and challenges. I'll share suggestions for recognizing and dealing with the red flags of life and how perfectionism can be dangerous to your health. We'll also explore how a goddess tests sincerity, learns to understand what it is she seeks, and how she gets smart with her heart in life and relationships.

Section Three is all about goddess wisdom on one of our favorite topics— MEN. I'll show you what to look for in an everyday hero, what attracts him, and why. We'll also break down the disappointments and workings of the heartbreaker and how to heed the red flags. (Special note: Some of you may be in relationships different from the male-female context described in this book. If so, that's fine—the goddess wisdom still applies!)

Section Four shows you how to surrender, let go and live! We'll review the importance of finding inner bliss and I'll summarize how you can begin right now!

Through this guide I hope to help you define who you are and kick up your confidence. I want to see you build a stronger you by not only envisioning your dream but living it. By shedding light on the challenging twists and turns that are a normal part of life, I encourage you to live realistically, mindfully, and blissfully. I want to help you lighten the baggage you've collected through life and teach you to reconfigure your automatic reactions, thereby reducing the frustration, stress and negativity that will steal your joy.

And last, but certainly not least, I encourage you to make the time to restore yourself, to build on positive thinking and behaving, and teach yourself to make time for simplicity and inner calm in your life.

Making life changes requires courage. Cleaning out the clutter in your mind, heart and life isn't an easy task. Though I can't personally be there with you, it is my hope that this book will guide you to make those changes that you may seek; that it will place you on the right track toward increasing your self-awareness and self-love. When we love ourselves, we are better able to effortlessly love others with more compassion. Life becomes more rewarding.

With motivation and courage I believe you can reinvent yourself to become an amazing, confident Urban Goddess. I have seen time and time again many clients transform their thinking, creating a more positive, fulfilling life. Finding your bliss and passion isn't always easy in an ever-changing, evolving universe. It is my hope that this book will give you the encouragement, inspiration and power to find your inner goddess wisdom and experience it.

Throughout your life, take time to pause and ask yourself: How is this working for me? If it's not working, have the courage to make the changes you seek.

What are you waiting for?

~Section One~
The Urban Goddess Lessons

The Urban Goddess knows that she is a precious diamond with many facets. She understands confidence means believing that you matter. If you want to make positive changes in your life, begin by changing the ordinary into the extraordinary. You are the artist of your masterpiece. You get to choose the colors and hues of your brushstrokes. With patience, understanding and desire, you can tap into your inner goddess wisdom by choosing smart heart choices that truly can transform your life.

Chapter One
The Urban Goddess Is Confident

"We delight in the beauty of the butterfly but rarely admit the changes it has gone through to achieve that beauty."
— Maya Angelou

As we begin the journey to find your inner bliss, I want you to know there is a simple, game-changing formula for unleashing the passionate, feisty, blissful, sensual, ageless goddess within you. To embrace her, you must get to know her and help her emerge. To unleash your inner goddess, you must find and define your authentic self by excavating the many complicated layers of your world.

Beauty Begins with Confidence

Your inner goddess has been there all along, but you may have been too distracted to notice her — until **now**.

Your **now** moment is when that quiet little voice grows loud enough that it cannot be ignored! The chic, bold, spirited goddess is in there and always has been there. Yet for her to fully be present, you must move past your disappointments, low self-esteem or worth, traumas and anxiety. You may never be completely cured of these banes, but I'm here to help you heal them, lighten the baggage and transform your thinking to view things in a different way. A calmer way. By learning to let go of these unfavorable traits, you permit yourself freedom of expression and can tap into your inner light of authenticity.

Goddess Pearls of Wisdom ...
"Beauty is how you feel inside and it reflects in your eyes.
It is not something physical." - Sophia Loren

Beauty begins in the mind and soul. It is the foundation built from the inside out creating magnificence, resilience and strength.

The Spell of Being in Vogue

Striving to be in vogue can be rather addicting. Billboards, talk shows, magazines, advertising and red carpet events are dripping with beauty, trends, fashion and ultimate lifestyles that keep many of us wanting to look better and have more.

The Urban Goddess has learned that she can appreciate life's indulgences but is not easily swayed.

Carrie Bradshaw, the character played by actress Sarah Jessica Parker in the television series *Sex and the City*, is the perfect example of a woman of substance and character I call an Urban Goddess. She marched to the beat of her own drum, she wrote about her life experiences and learned her own lessons, albeit painfully at times. Her obsession with designer shoes and the ambivalent Mr. Big helped her become a household name and many women related to her role.

What so many of us loved about the Carrie Bradshaw character was that she was so real. Authentic, unique, vulnerable and feisty.

There are few women who do not seek a lifestyle filled with meaning, sensuality, desire, beauty, and uniqueness. Unfortunately the media, fashion and beauty worlds often have a tremendous influence on us and not always in a positive way.

This is not to say that buying a new pair of shoes, shopping away at Sephora, or buying a designer dress at Bergdorf's that sets you back a paycheck is always dangerous. Indulgence is fine, within reason, but self-control is key. There is a good amount of truth in the saying, "Too much of a good thing can be dangerous." If every time you feel stressed, down or frustrated you binge on food, shopping, alcohol or other substances, they may temporarily calm the anxiety but it is a quick fix. Similar to putting a Band-Aid on a large wound.

Being in vogue, trendy, and fashionable, or striving to look years younger as we grow older can all be healthy habits, but can also become an unhealthy obsession unless we keep it in check and keep it real.

It seems that everywhere we turn, everywhere we look, so many of us are trying too hard to look too perfect. We start off wanting to be admired or appreciated for our uniqueness yet often get caught up in doing the very things that mimic the rest of the crowd. We become spellbound by fancy advertising and hype.

How many little black dresses or pearls do we really need? How many bottles of skin care products are necessary?

Yet when the dresses fray, the jewels tarnish and our crow's feet return — as they always do — how do feel then? Are temporary "fixes" the answer to permanent bliss? Is there such thing as the right amount of self-indulgence?

Do these things truly make us feel more beautiful?

I believe that if an indulgence will truly make you feel better and you are not doing anything inherently dangerous, then some cosmetic beauty enhancements and/or a closet full of Dior may not be all bad — as long as you can afford it, of course.

You can be in vogue, fashionable and look great by making smart, heartfelt goddess choices. Be true to yourself. Think before you act. Challenge your thoughts then listen to your inner guidance and feel secure in your choices.

Gain Immediate Confidence

The first key to developing confidence is to take responsibility for your life. Believe that you're in charge of your life. Though others may want to help (which is awesome, but...) learn to depend on YOU!

You can have the most fabulous things in the universe and the most awesome people in your life, but if YOU aren't happy within yourself, none of those things or people is going to make you happy. They can only complement and enhance what's already inside of you.

The Urban Goddess is always searching for ways to improve, learn and grow. She reminds herself life is not measured by the attitude of or interaction with others who do not speak from a place of authenticity or a higher good. She can stand proudly on her own two feet! She is open to compromise and communication but never sells herself short of her worth!

Times can be tough. Backward steps are sometimes out of our control. We trip up, fall and get up again. The Urban Goddess learns to stop blaming the world but goes out and makes the change she seeks.

A confident Urban Goddess knows that she is good enough.

She listens to others when they speak. She respects others. She respects herself. She chooses to make changes and improvements in her own life. If she feels someone close to her would benefit from an improvement, change, or some insight she can offer, she does not force, but instead, she suggests and encourages. She knows she **cannot change another person** until they are ready and ripe for change. She **accepts people for who they are.** If that doesn't work for her, she learns to distance or move on.

An Urban Goddess is not a victim

An Urban Goddess is never afraid to open another door, to let go and surrender when needed, or to experience uncertainty for period of time. She has studied and mastered her natural gift of intuitive guidance and utilizes it.

She exemplifies a living legend in her actions.

She trusts her judgment.

> *"Confidence is the key to success (in life, in love, in everything!). One of the best ways to gain more confidence is to reach out and help others. Being confident improves how we look, feel and act. In order to achieve, we must believe in ourselves. It makes the journey worthwhile." – Jaclyn Zukerman*

Chapter Two
The Urban Goddess Emotional Beauty Toobox

"Outer beauty attracts but inner beauty captivates."
~ Kate Angell

Every seasoned goddess (or goddess in training) knows that having an amazing beauty bag is a must! A great lipstick, bronzer compact and a tinted moisturizer keep us fresh and looking good. Our hairdressers and colorists are often on speed dial since great hair is … well, a must-have!

Looking beautiful, well-groomed and polished are signs of good self-esteem. Looking good does not mean that you need to look perfect. It does not mean that you need to dress to the nines to be sophisticated and classy. Looking beautiful is more, much more, than that. A great deal of beauty is reflected from the inside out. The Urban Goddess keeps it simple, keeps it real and effortlessly sprinkles her life with passion.

Internal beauty will radiate externally and create an instant aura of confidence and fabulousness. Therefore, it's important for every Urban Goddess to have an emotional beauty toolbox. More important, even, than that essential beauty bag.

The following is a list of tools and thoughts that should be in every well-stocked emotional toolbox:

- Patience.
- Confidence.
- Keep it real.
- Keep it simple.
- Keep it classy.
- Be true to you.
- Be sensual and passionate.
- Don't sweat the small stuff....ever.
- "No" is a complete sentence — use it when necessary.
- From the way you dress, to the way you walk and talk, be your unique self, always.
- When God closes a door, he opens a window.
- Find soothing ways to relax and decompress to reduce stress.
- Don't try to control every detail.
- Speak your mind, and then learn to let things go.
- Pray.
- Meditate.
- Be of service and help to make the world a better place.

Take responsibility for and charge of your life. Do not blame others for the difficulties in your life. You can share them with a trusted person, and even be angry about unfairness, but never adopt a victim mentality!

Remember: You can have the most fabulous things in the universe and the most awesome people who love you, but if you aren't happy with yourself, not one of those things or people is going to make you feel happy.

If you aren't in charge of your life, start making changes today!

The Urban Goddess knows that times can be tough. Sometimes two steps forward and a step backward may be out of her control, but as soon as she sways off course, she steers herself back!

The Urban Goddess has learned that being in harmony and balance with her sense of self is one of life's greatest gifts. In order to get there she must step into the unknown. A tiptoe and then a giant leap of faith.

Goddess Pearls of Wisdom ...

"I believe in manicures. I believe in overdressing. I believe in primping at leisure and wearing lipstick. I believe in pink. I believe happy girls are the prettiest girls. I believe that tomorrow is another day and I believe in miracles." – Audrey Hepburn

How a Goddess radiates her beauty

She embraces her feminine mystique.

She delights in the wonder of who she is.

She encompasses a beautiful heart, mind and soul.

She smiles often, which radiates her face and will make her eyes sparkle.

Being rude and insensitive has no place in the goddess energy. Being sassy, quick humored, totally acceptable!

The Urban Goddess knows she is a constant work in progress. She is in harmony with her mind, body, and spirit, and she is curious and always learning here in the earth school.

She releases negative thoughts as often as possible. When her inner bitch, dark swan emerges, she monitors her stay. Jealousy, envy, drama, extreme narcissism and selfishness have no place in the life of a woman of substance. She uses self-discipline to think mindfully with beautiful thoughts.

The goddess cultivates her beauty even in the small things and most simple interactions.

She incorporates self-care daily. She is well pulled together before she walks out the door. Her exterior is a reflection of how she feels on the inside.

If she doesn't have time for makeup, she learns to smile a lot!

She makes the time to research and read about people that inspire her and the world. She loves to read because she knows it will increase her knowledge of the world that surrounds her.

She is creative in thought and in heart with style and grace.

The Urban Goddess surrounds herself with beauty

As you continue on your journey to unleash your Urban Goddess and ignite her dreams and passions, you will naturally want to fill your environment with beauty, serenity, sweetness and bling. Learn to put your footprint on what surrounds you. It will help define you.

Simple touches can have a tremendous, positive impact on your life. Your environment is one critical component of your Urban Goddess mentality and lifestyle.

Keep your home — especially your bedroom — and your office filled with simple treasures that bring you beauty and joy. Beautiful soft hues and colors, vases, bling picture frames, vintage lampshades, antique pieces and art can fill your home and work environment with your own unique and delicious personality. Browse Pinterest and home décor magazines, or attend Feng Shui workshops to learn about your environment and its effect on relaxation.

Simple ways to create bliss in your environment

Create an environment filled with things that you love and inspire you. You do not need the most expensive furniture or trinkets to create a blissful environment. You only need things that are beautiful to YOU.

Be creative and patient. Once you have a vision of what you love, take your time incorporating those items into your home and office. Let your blissful environment evolve.

Recite metaphors to motivate yourself. Think good thoughts. Prioritize balance daily. Be sure to have your environment in line with your energy. Peace, serenity, beauty.

Work by soft lighting. Just as we all look better in candlelight, soft lighting at the office helps you feel more relaxed, and causes less squinting and headaches. Buy a lamp for work and use soft lighting at home.

Picture frames are such a simple way to incorporate art or photography in your office and home décor, and beautiful frames are easy to find. Fill them with photos, quotes and art depicting things that you love and inspire you.

How often do you bask in life's simple pleasures?

Basking in life's simple pleasures can bring joy and serenity to your world.

By taking a moment to stop and be mindful of the moment, you can drastically improve your mood and thought process. Here are some ways that can help get you started:

- Absorbing a gentle, cool breeze.

- Listening to the sounds of the ocean.

- Walking barefoot in the sand.

- Walking barefoot through the grass.

- Taking a walk or hike in nature.

- Visiting an animal shelter and giving hugs.

- Reading a great book that inspires you.

- Sipping a smooth, warm latte while sitting by a fire.

- Having a cool drink on a hot summer's day.

- Watching a funny movie and laughing (a lot!).

- Helping a senior cross the street.

- Meditate just to relax.

- Get a massage, just because!

- Place fresh flowers in your room.

- Take a drive through the country.

- Visit a vintage or antique shop.

- Write a letter — with a pen and paper!

- Watch the sun rise and set.

- Sleep in on a rainy day and not feel guilty.

- Create a vision board of your future. Collect photos, magazine ads and quotes of the things that really matter to you. Post it somewhere where you can reflect on it daily.

Intuition

Listen. Do you hear that small, still voice inside of you? Perhaps it's in the form of an instinctive **knowing** or a flash feeling. This is a natural, invisible gift, outside our rational thought process, that's been used by goddesses throughout history. Even ancient goddesses knew how to trust their intuition. If you become aware of it and learn to understand its message, you can allow intuition to help guide you.

Ask yourself: Do you **feel** balanced or off-balanced around a particular person or in certain situations?

Do you **sense** something is off? Do you feel at peace and in harmony with a particular person?

What does your body **feel** when you are around a particular person?

Your guidance system could very well be warning you or encouraging you about a particular person or situation. **Pay attention.**

Many people, when they want to know more about a person, company, group, or organization, will do Internet research to collect helpful information. Do not hesitate to do this! But learn to trust your intuition as well.

Tap into your intuition

Tapping into your intuition means that you will need to step outside your logical, linear mindset. Our minds are continually processing thoughts and information, so this won't be easy, but can be learned.

Here are some tips to get you started.

Allow yourself some quiet time, free from distractions. Relax your body and close your eyes. Take several deep breaths, then gradually relax your breathing.

Feel a sense of peace for several minutes. Visualize a beautiful place, and sit with it for a few moments, focusing on your breath.

Once you're relaxed and your mind is clear, ask yourself a question that is important to you. See if an answer comes to you naturally and effortlessly. If not, be patient. The answer will come to you soon. Be in touch with feelings, events, sensations, dreams that may give you some insight.

With practice, you can learn to tap into your intuition and trust its guidance, to the point it becomes automatic.

Inspiration

Inspiration is a power that helps us stretch and soar to new heights. By exploring what inspires us, we begin to feel more alive, more motivated. We set higher expectations for ourselves. We begin to understand what drives us, what makes us thrive, what moves us, shakes us, and rocks our world.

We may be inspired by a friend, a mentor, a teacher, a story, an organization, a group, a pet, a hero. Inspiration may have different meanings to us at different chapters in our lives.

Urban Goddess Thoughts on Inspiration

Inspiration. A word that describes putting meaning and passion into our world.

A confident Urban Goddess is one that is often inspired, even by the most simple details of daily life.

Become more curious and fascinated by the unfolding of daily life. Bask in the joy of a sunny, warm day or savoring the delight of a decadent dessert.

Inspiration can also be much more profound. Feeling the chills of wonder in a special song. Listening mindfully to a prolific motivational speech or resonating with the story line of a movie. My father once told me that having something to look forward to and feel rewarded by makes life worth living.

Whatever inspires you will help you in your daily life, to be a constant work in progress. So often we let life take charge of us instead of us taking charge of our own lives. We may not be able to stop the clock from ticking but we can stop ourselves from constantly looking at it.

Have you ever had a moment where time seemed to stand still? Or at least you wish it did?

Often that is a moment when you were fully present. You were naturally being mindful of living in that moment.

You cannot force yourself to be inspired but you can begin the journey to become more aware of what you enjoy, what makes you smile and brings harmony and happiness to you.

Thinking about what inspires you is a good start, but beginning to manifest it to the next step is key.

When you incorporate inspiration it becomes the difference between waking up and just getting through the day or waking up and getting a step closer to living with purpose.

Inspiration is powerful. It's readily available, and in endless supply if we only seek it out or watch for it. Inspiration can propel you to be or do the things you've always dreamed of; it can motivate you to take action to make the world a better place; it can help you develop courage. And, it's one of the most potent ingredients you can use to develop confidence and inner beauty.

Get Inspired Now

Write, be creative, and get in touch with your artsy side.

Serve. There is nothing as rewarding as giving to others who are in need. Everyone has something to give.

Be authentic. Speak as if you matter. Listen as if others matter to you.

Do something out of your comfort zone. Draw, paint, cook a new dish, dance, sing, laugh for no reason, smile at everyone you encounter.

Listen to your favorite music every day.

Meditate. Mediation is truly one of the greatest gifts we can give ourselves on a daily basis. It is that special place that you can bask in the peace of just "being."

Work out. Join a gym, yoga class, run, or walk. Get out there and get moving. No excuses!

Your relationship with yourself

Renowned psychotherapist Rollo May was one of the few experts in the field of psychology that helped us better understand the importance of learning and strengthening one's sense of self. According to May, a person's level of self-esteem and self-awareness will affect every single aspect and relationship of their life.

The stronger your sense of self, the more authentic a relationship you will have with yourself. You will then begin to naturally reflect that inner beauty, confidence and love of self to others. It will naturally radiate from the inside out. There is such a thing as healthy narcissism. It is a healthy sense of entitlement. Do not confuse it with being selfish!

Take the time to nurture your body temple, because it is the house of your body, soul, mind, and spirit. Tap into your body's needs. What are the things that nourish your body? What makes it feel good, sensual, and beautiful? Take the time to tap into what makes you feel "less than" at times. Learn to encourage yourself. You get to choose your mood!

Relationships are our bloodlines. We need others and others need us, but we need to love ourselves in order to have healthy relationships. We must learn not to be afraid to be alone, to revel in our own company. We must learn not to be afraid but to enjoy autonomy, serenity and peacefulness in solitude.

Relationships are part of our daily existence and many of them add value and love to our lives. Some relationships do not. We need to be acutely aware of those unhealthy relationships. We must challenge our thoughts, and pay careful attention to others' actions and the feelings they create within us.

Learn to have a healthy relationship with yourself. Support, love and encourage yourself. Only permit others who encourage you entry into your mind, world and body temple. Ride the waves only with those who are willing to ride them with you. Never force.

Chapter Three
The Urban Goddess Is a Peaceful Warrior

"You had the power all along my dear."
~ Glenda the Good Witch

The Urban Goddess is a peaceful warrior. She spreads love, joy, kindness and nurture. She also knows how to kick up her heels, let go, speak her mind. She possesses self-esteem, not selfishness. She feels a healthy sense of entitlement. The Peaceful Warrior is comfortable in her own skin.

She honors herself and others by knowing the crucial role of people's personal space, as well as her own.

She works on her individual growth and personal development.

She has healthy expectations — of others, of life, and of herself.

Ways to tap into your peaceful warrior

Don't be afraid to take inventory of your life.

Learn to let go of what no longer serves you.

Find ways to accept change and uncertainty. Research and read about how other people conquered these fears.

Expect 100% relationships, not 50/50. Emotionally intelligent people are whole people, not halves in search of another half to "complete" them or "fix" them. You want a whole person as a friend, lover, companion, family member.

The Peaceful Warrior Goddess is excited about exploring all she can be and isn't afraid to take a leap of faith.

She is courageous. She knows the outcomes will be worth the challenges.

Goddess Pearls of Wisdom ...

"Sometimes you must go through extremely hard experiences to get you to a good place. Confidence begins by believing in you. When you believe in yourself you are capable of anything you dream of being. Trust in what you believe to be right, trust in what makes you happy and trust in what you don't understand. That is how you gain knowledge and expansion." – Laura Zukerman

Begin each day with mindful intention

The Peaceful Warrior Goddess is also intentional, so make it a practice to set your intentions daily. They can be simple or complex but take a few moments to acknowledge them and journal them. Start with the day, then the week, and if you like, move further into the future.

Meditate. Mindful meditation, simple yoga stretches, or a walk through the park or near a body of water are exercises that can help clear your mind to see things more clearly.

Stretch your body. Close your eyes, and breathe deeply and meaningfully for several minutes. This will provide you energy to start your day.

Do not overload your schedule. Allow yourself time gaps in between appointments, events, or meetings so that you can decompress. It is essential to keep your stress levels low to feel energized throughout the day.

Begin a sensual journey. Learn to become more aware of and in touch with your body. Sensual women are more confident, enjoy pleasure, have more orgasms and radiate passion.

Do not compare yourself to others. While it is normal and natural to sometimes feel competitive, less than, disappointed in yourself, or not good enough, do not let these feelings drive your thoughts. Train and discipline your mind so that whenever you get one of these thoughts you remind yourself that there is only one unique you, so it is a waste of time to compare yourself with anyone. We may all have similarities but there is only one unique you!

Learn to trust your judgment and intuition, and STOP always questioning yourself. Pay attention to the signs and feelings you experience. Trust that your perceptions are often right on track. If you doubt yourself, ask a trusted friend or mentor for their thoughts.

When life gets complicated and confusing, be patient and keep trusting your judgment and intuition. With time and patience, you will get the answers you need. You may never get all the answers you want, but rest assured — you will get the answers you need!

Try not to overanalyze your life. I know how hard this is. I was guilty of this one myself, especially being a counselor! Learn to let things go sometimes.

You are not alone. You may experience loneliness or sadness after a loss or major transition — that is a normal part of life, but you never have to be alone. The loneliness will pass quickly once you have developed and cultivated the strong sense of self that you aspire to. You may find it helpful to explore and develop new coping skills such as resilience and self-soothing. Seek out support groups, counseling groups, or even workshops, which are available in almost every city around the country. Counseling centers and religious organizations are wonderful resources for support when you're coping with loss, grief, or even major life changes.

The Urban Goddess knows how to take care of herself. She indulges herself (her mind and body temple), but is smart about it. She knows that she is worthy of looking good, feeling good and being treated well!

The Urban Goddess enjoys serving her country, her family, those she loves, her community, and others. She is a woman of fearless, infinite passion, and she knows there is nothing more satisfying than the incredible reward that comes from giving to others and loving others who need her help. Sometimes even the smallest gesture can mean a great deal to someone else.

> *"You, more than anybody else, deserve your own love and affection."* — *Buddha*

The Urban Goddess knows how to say "no" but when she can say "yes" she helps to make the world a better place.

The Goddess Knows You Never Give Up

We sometimes need to make courageous choices. Some days even small choices or small challenges can feel overwhelming if we are tired, stressed, or feeling under the weather.

Goddesses find the courage to face choices and challenges. They find that one twinkle in the star even when the chips are down. A universal truth is better to believe that all will be okay, because if we manifest good and wonder, then good and wonder will head our way.

The Urban Goddess knows that tomorrow is another day. So what if today wasn't as perfect as it could have been? There is always tomorrow.

You always have a choice. You can choose to move forward or you can stay where you are. Develop the habit of asking yourself: How is this working for me? You can choose to rejoice in your blessings and keep moving forward or complain about what hasn't worked for you and waste time. In the Urban Goddess world, there is no time to complain! Goddess girls get moving.

You always have the freedom to walk away, to change the outcome, to change yourself.

Chapter Four
The Urban Goddess Is Sensual

"God gave women intuition and femininity. Used properly, the combination easily jumbles the brain of any man I've ever met."
~ Farrah Fawcett

The Urban Goddess is a sassy girl wrapped in a package of class, style, grace, smarts and heart. She has a burning desire to live life agelessly and deliciously.

How to Embrace and Ignite Your Urban Goddess Sensuality

Every Urban Goddess has a passionate, feisty approach to life balanced by a softness that draws others to her like a moth to a flame. Her warmth and presence are contagious. Most people find her intriguing, yet she also is very transparent. She effortlessly moves through life with psychological swank and mystique. She is in touch with her wisdom and inner bitch, yet she is empathetic towards others.

Being sensual is living completely, totally, divinely, deliciously. It is accepting and embracing special moments and riding the waves of challenge, adversity and uncertainty.

The Urban Goddess knows that she can be fascinating and still authentic. Not all Urban Goddesses are born with a strong sense of self. Often it is learned behavior, and the Urban Goddess masters it.

Sex is a beautiful thing under the right circumstances and shared with a special someone. It can be hot, passionate, soft and tender, rough and raw, depending on the mood and circumstances. Sex is a wonderful way to share love and desire with another. Of course, it can also be used as a great stress reducer!

Sex isn't always about love, though it often can be. For the sake of emotional and physical safety, it is best to have sex only with someone you trust, someone you feel very attracted to, and someone you know well.

It may seem hot and bad-girlish to have sex with a guy you only met hours before, but Urban Goddesses are smarter than that. They live that fantasy turn-on only in steamy romance novels, but in real life they get to know someone before they take off their clothes.

You can have amazing, fireworks sex when you feel good about your body. So many women have body image issues which substantially decreases the chances of a woman feeling passionate and being great in bed. The woman with body issues will be so worried about whether her breasts are sagging or her hips are too big that she will miss out on all the fun! Men love to be with women who love their bodies and feel good about themselves. You do not have to have a perfect body in order to feel beautiful and sensual. Not all Urban Goddesses have a perfect body, but they master the art of being sensual!

Learn to look at yourself in the mirror, flaws and all, and rejoice in the amazing, unique body you have. If there are things you don't love about yourself, learn to accept them. But if a few extra pounds are keeping you from loving your body, working out a bit more or eating a more balanced diet can help build muscle and keep you shapely and sexy. Working out is always smart, as it increases the endorphins in your body, which will boost your self-esteem.

Remember: super-thin is not the way to go, nor is being overweight. You want to feel good and look good. Take pride in your appearance, exercise and eat healthy.

Five Urban Goddess keys to a sexier, more sensual you

One: The best sex happens where there is a connection of mind, body and spirit. If you are unsure of someone, do not sleep with them. Take the time to get to know someone you're attracted to. Always have safe sex. Why? Because a goddess is smart with her heart. She knows that she will become bonded to a partner who may not be suitable for her. She understands that she needs to protect her emotions and her body from unnecessary harm and disease. Be sexy, sensual and smart!

Learn to love your body, flaws and all. There are all kinds of beautiful shapes, sizes and dimensions. Learn to be happy with the gifts you have been given and flaunt them!

Two: Live in the moment and bask in the joy of today. Living in the moment helps you thoroughly enjoy each moment you are given. Your sexual life will be enhanced by you being fully present.

Three: Sex is not only body-to-body touching. Becoming a sexier you starts in the brain. Remind yourself daily how beautiful and sexy you are. As you do, you will begin to feel it and believe it.

Four: Be in touch with your body temple. Know what feels good, what pleases you. Free yourself from inhibitions.

Five: Be intuitive about sexual partners.

Do not compare yourself to others! Learn to become more aware and in touch with your body and sensations of what brings you pleasure and joy. Sensual women who are in touch with their senses, feelings and body are more confident, enjoy more intense pleasure. They are naturally passionate.

The Urban Goddess Thoughts on the Allure of Mystique

Many books, blogs, websites and seminars claim the way to snag a guy is to "be a bitch," play his game, be unavailable most of the time, don't answer his calls and basically drive him crazy.

Of course it is very exciting to have a man that you are crazy about be crazy about you too. But, contrary to the advice of those dating experts, you do not want to drive a man crazy for too long. The reason is, every man at some point in their lives — especially when they fall in love with a woman— want a woman who is REAL. A woman that is beautiful but who knows what she wants, tells it like it is, and keeps the man on his toes.

Unfortunately, not all people have good intentions. Some may toy with your emotions. There are those who run hot and cold, love you, love you not, may be prone to abandonment and betrayal, may have a personality disorder such as narcissism, or are generally emotionally unhealthy. Playing along with this game may be exciting and intriguing at first, but over time YOU will drive YOURSELF insane. Over time a relationship like this takes its toll on your emotional and physical health and eventually it will become too stressful to remain with this person. The end result is usually nasty breakups, spitefulness, anger, disappointment and a great deal of unnecessary heartbreak.

If you get into a relationship, it is YOUR responsibility to make certain you know what you want, what the other person wants, and whether you can both make that work together. If not, GET OUT EARLY. Do not remain in a relationship out of fear of being alone, guilt, and/or fear of hurting feelings. Easier said than done, but choose emotional health.

The best way to intrigue the partner of your dreams is to believe you deserve to be treated well.

Treat yourself well and others will treat you similarly!

Love yourself, love others, do the things you love to do.

Don't give up everything for a man. Always make sure you stay you, but do treat him like a king if you love him. He will in turn treat you like his queen. If he doesn't, you may want to rethink your relationship. Relationships are not always a bed of roses, but if your bed is full of thorns, it may be best to toss it!

Remember, if it's not working, don't keep trying to work it out. Give the relationship a time limit and move on if you need to.

The Power of No

Some people have difficulty with the word *no*.

Yet the word no is a complete sentence and doesn't require an elaborate explanation. Saying the word no is sometimes important. Sometimes you just need a break. Alone time. Are really busy and can't help someone out, again.

Using the word no is a great way to simplify your life. Some people will not like it when you say no to them. They may say or do manipulative things in order to get you to say yes. Don't be easily swayed. Unless it is an emergency, don't feel you always have to say yes.

Use the word no when necessary.

No is especially necessary when dealing with a toxic, difficult personality.

The truth is, there are some people who are toxic to us and have poor boundaries. They expect us to take care of them even at the expense of losing ourselves in the process.

Five Ways the Urban Goddess Learns When to Say NO:

One: When someone is overstepping boundaries and you feel taken advantage of.

Two: If you feel physical symptoms that make you ill or uncomfortable. Your gut feelings and intuition will guide you when you should say no to a particular person or situation.

Three: If a particular person or group of persons have asked you repeatedly to do things for them with little, if any, reciprocity. There is no give and take.

Four: You feel drained, stressed, tired, sick.

Five: You have said yes all your life and now just want to say, HELL NO!

Perfectionism

A perfect body, a perfect job, a perfect life, and huge financial success. This may be the motto of many ad campaigns, corporate CEOs, air-brushed magazine covers and motivational gurus, but the truth is, perfectionism can be dangerous to your health. Instead, strive to be perfectly imperfect at times. There is always another day and time to improve.

Perfectionism is quite different from striving to be your best self. Your best self may enjoy a challenge, a race or competition. Perfectionism can seem harmless, yet it causes many people to feel overwhelmed, stressed, less than, disappointed, angry and depressed. In some extreme cases it causes suicide ideation. The reason is, no matter how far you try to reach for perfection in all areas of your life, you will often not succeed. Why? Because your life will be out of balance when the scales are tipped. **Learn to slow down!** Not everything in life has to be a race or competition.

It is impossible to relax when you're stressed. In order to stay at the top on all you do, you often have to make sacrifices. So if you stay longer hours at work or on a project, then your family/children suffer because you are neglecting time with them. You are also neglecting down time for yourself. Remember you must replenish yourself daily. **Rest, relax, restore is the motto of the Urban Goddess.**

Perfectionism often causes a great deal of anger and frustration. It can cause eating disorders, addiction issues, emotional imbalance and other health issues.

Be aware if you tend to be a perfectionist. Think about opting for the best you can be while being mindful of your health, your quality of life and life balance.

Ask yourself the following questions to see if you tend towards perfectionism:

- If I don't set high standards for myself, I will fail.
- I feel ashamed or humiliated when I feel weak or emotional.
- I need to punish myself when I don't live up to my own expectations.
- I must be able to be great at anything and everything.
- If I can't win or be the best at something, why bother?

Examine the language you use. When you use all-or-nothing language such as *I will, I can't, I must, I need, I don't,* you set yourself up for disappointment.

Chapter Five
The Urban Goddess and the Inner Goddess Muse

"People will forget what you said. People will forget what you did, but people will never forget how you made them feel."
— Maya Angelou

Many artists will tell you their inspiration comes from their muse. Not only artists, but musicians, writers, photographers, designers, leaders, motivational speakers, coaches, teachers, counselors, and even clergy.

A muse is a force of inspiration. When you admire a beautiful work of art, a photograph, a magnificent building or garden, have you ever wondered what inspired its creator? Learn to "wonder" more. Tap into your intuitive feelings. We all have an inner muse. If you would like to ignite your inner muse, learn to tune into the feelings, sensations, emotions and experiences of each of the roles you play in your daily life.

In Greek mythology, the god Zeus and goddess Mnemosyne had nine daughters who were all muses.

- Calliope, Goddess of Epic Poetry

- Clio, Goddess of History

- Erato, Goddess of lyric Poetry

- Euterpe, Goddess of Music

- Melpomene, Goddess of Tragedy

- Polyhymnia, Goddess of Sacred Music

- Terpsichore, Goddess of Dance and Song

- Thalea, Goddess of Comedy

- Urania, Goddess of Astronomy

Goddess history and inspiration is becoming all the rage these days, and for good reason. Throughout the ages, goddesses inspired women legends with their philosophy, mystique and inner guidance. Today, you can find groups around the country that offer courses, lessons, workshops and lectures on the history and mythology of the ancient goddesses. Explore your curiosity and see where it leads you.

Ways the Urban Goddess Can Unleash Her Inner Muse

Collect, recite and repeat affirmations that inspire you daily.

Be more passionate — about life, love, nature, living in the moment.

Listen to your heart but make decisions with your mind and soul.

Nourish your body temple. Share your knowledge with others.

Be grateful. Every day. Perhaps you've seen the quote, "Enjoy the little things in life because one day when you look back, you will realize they were the big things." How true that is.

Incorporate daily meditation. Be mindful of the tastes, sounds, and touch around you. Marvel in the magnificence of the world you were born into.

Create your own personal space with style, grace, and heart. Learn to leave your fingerprint on all you do, in your own unique way.

Learn about Feng Shui. Feng Shui is the ancient Chinese art of placement, discovered over 3,000 years ago. Many believe that this art helps to balance our energy along with the universe, creating positive energy and vibrations around our homes and environment.

Have a plan for dealing with stress. For example, decide ahead of time that when stressed, you will meditate, take a nap, walk the dog, take a run.

By taking just a few minutes each day to make a plan or jot down ideas, you can save time and reduce your stress.

Chapter Six
The Urban Goddess and the Inner Bitch

"I can define bitch. It's a babe in total control of herself."
~ Star Jones

We've now covered some important lessons for developing the Urban Goddess within you; lessons focused on strengthening your heart and letting your inner goddess beauty shine.

- Stocking your emotional beauty toolbox.

- Mastering the word *no*.

- Developing your inner confidence.

In order to be confident, you need to understand and develop both your light and dark sides. So, while the Urban Goddess knows how to develop her inner beauty, she also knows to respect and embrace her inner bitch.

I want to challenge you to ignite your inner bitch and surrender to the feisty goddess within!

Ready to take that next leap of goddess faith? Ready to ignite your inner bitch and learn not to fear her? This is accomplished by having complete control and knowing how to tame her.

Igniting your inner bitch is not difficult at all, because unless you are Mother Teresa or some other saint (nothing personal, but chances are you and I are not!), we all have a level of feistiness within us and occasionally get angry.

In order to continue on your confident, sassy, classy goddess journey, you will now need to introduce yourself to your darker side and not fear her!

You will want to polish your bitch skills. You can tame and train your inner bitch so that she appears when needed and appropriate.

How to Ignite Your Urban Goddess Inner Bitch

One: Limit but embrace the Lioness. Know that the Inner Bitch speaks her mind but is not a loud, obnoxious diva or drama queen.

Two: In touch. The Inner Bitch is one part of a beautiful woman who is in touch with all parts of her light and dark sides.

Three: Respect. Women who are confident and in touch with their authentic selves learn not to fear their dark bitch side but respect her opinion.

Four: The dark shadow, as described by therapist Carl Jung, is the part of us that is resilient and fearless. A part that can speak her mind, believes her voice counts and has mastered the sexiness, hotness and strength of her feminine power.

Five: Tame her. The most important element to embracing the bitch in you is to always have her under your control and to tame her.

Six: Monitor her stay. There is always an appropriate time and place for the Inner Bitch to take center stage. Like the black swan, she can be selfish and greedy. Do not let her overstay her welcome.

Seven: You always have options and choices. Your strategies for dealing with joy, anger, fear, and frustration can be embraced and tamed. Don't lose sight of that.

Eight: Become aware of your triggers. Sometimes the Inner Bitch will just show up because she handled things for you in the past. It may be an automatic response. You can change how you react to a situation by doing something as incredibly simple as taking a deep breath before you say or do anything. It's a small habit that can make all the difference in the world.

Nine: We all have a dual nature. Some of us are just better able to control the energy we expend on each part of it.

Ten: Healthy narcissism. Igniting Your Inner Bitch is really a metaphor for standing up for yourself and what you believe. It represents a healthy dose of narcissism.

The well-rounded Urban Goddess who understands and embraces both her light and dark sides will:

❧ Feel good about herself.

❧ Let her voice be heard.

❧ Set boundaries and back them up.

❧ Give off good energy and surround herself with others who have similar vibrational energies.

❧ Live by The Golden Rule and treat others as she would want to be treated.

❧ Learn and grow her mind daily. Embrace her light and dark sides.

The Urban Goddess Lesson on Life's Twists and Turns

In this section we will explore the various workings of uncertainty and change.

Since change is constant throughout our lives, it is important to be prepared for the uncertainty it may bring. Though it is difficult to predict what the future will hold, having thought through different scenarios in your mind as to how you would react is helpful.

Prepare to have some alternative plans for your life. You may never need to use them, but it is helpful to at least think things through from different perspectives. This way, if the time comes that you need to make a sudden change or are facing a difficult challenge or uncertainty, you will be better equipped to handle a situation if life throws you a curve ball!

Chapter Seven
The Urban Goddess Is Smart with Her Heart

"You see a lot of smart guys with dumb women, but you hardly ever see a smart woman with a dumb guy."

~ Erica Jong

An Urban Goddess knows it is important to have a smart heart in all she does but especially when it comes to relationships. Unfortunately, life being what it is, not everyone has good intentions. Living your life positively is one thing but deluding yourself is quite another.

It is your choice and yours alone to get smart with your heart. Urban Goddess wisdom can point you down the right path but only you can choose your actions. When your mind is clear — out of the fog — you will have the emotional tools to construct stronger boundaries with difficult and toxic people. Toxic people can be hazardous to your emotional and physical health. Do not underestimate the destruction that they can cause to your sense of well-being and esteem.

An Urban Goddess **observes behavior and sets boundaries** for what is and isn't acceptable behavior. A boundary shows a strong sense of self and esteem. It is a line you draw in the sand of what and what is not acceptable to you. In order to have a healthy relationship, it is important to have boundaries and share what they are. It is just as important to enforce those boundaries. If someone doesn't respect your boundaries, you may want to rethink the relationship.

If you're struggling with a relationship or a difficult situation, ask yourself the following questions:

❧ How am I feeling in this moment?

❧ How am I feeling with this person?

❧ How am I feeling in this relationship?

❧ What energy level do I feel this person is at?

❧ What is my energy level when I am with this person?

If you are in a relationship with this person, are you genuinely happy most of the time or do they often drain you? (This is what experts often refer to as toxic relationships.)

Observe their body language. Do they seem relaxed around you? Do they seem tense or uneasy? Do you feel relaxed around this person or do you feel uneasy?

Is this often, or only on rare occasions?

Use reflective listening. Mirror what they say so you understand and they feel heard.

This is a good starting point to see where you are at or heading in a particular relationship. **Balance is very important.**

Once your self-awareness and confidence are stronger, you will be able to decode the red flags of toxic people and relationships. It will become more natural to you.

The choices you make today can be healthier than those you have made in the past. We often make choices based on our level of intention or energy at that time in our lives.

You will see clearly as you walk out of the fog that the red flags are either there or not. Sometimes you may think you see red flags that aren't really there. A weak sense of self or diminished confidence may cause you to imagine red flags where they really don't exist, so remember the importance of a strong sense of self. But legitimate red flags are warnings that something is off. It can be a sudden jolt or thought. A flash feeling that something isn't quite right. It can also be a "right in your face" comment or action. It almost always is worth it to delve a little deeper if you sense a red flag.

When you come from a place of strength and esteem, you learn to decipher more easily between a character disturbance and someone who is emotionally intelligent and balanced, but may be going through a rough time.

Remember to ask yourself: How is this working for me? What changes can I make to improve myself or my situation?

Unlock your feminine smarts to strengthen the inner core of your sense of self. You do this by forcing yourself to excavate all that is inside of you and over time, mold and shape your inner goddess.

The very essence of who you are and what you believe, feel, and incorporate into your life play a vital role in your life choices.

By building a stronger foundation and trusting your perceptions, your choices in a partner, career, and friendships will be greatly impacted by the level of confidence you have in yourself.

Jealousy

Jealousy occurs in varying degrees. It runs on a spectrum from mild to moderate to out-of-control jealous paranoia.

There is NO question that if you ever suspect you are being abused by a jealous, controlling person that you **seek help immediately.**

It is also important to pay attention to your own jealous feelings and reactions. Become aware of your triggers and automatic reactions. Ask yourself when you are calmer if this is something that may be rooted in your past that hasn't been dealt with and processed. If you can honestly admit that you often have reactions that may be automatic and dramatic it is time to work on improving how you communicate these reactions. Of course, sometimes a bit of jealousy is warranted. Try to communicate your feelings constructively. Observe if this person is willing to work with you to assuage your fears or concerns. If not, you may need to rethink the relationship.

Jealousy, in its early stages, or in the mild to moderate form, may appear benign but ends up becoming rather dangerous to your emotional health and welfare. Jealousy, except on rare occasion and in its mildest forms, is called the green-eyed monster for a reason. It is bad. It is dangerous. It will destroy your spirit. It can kill you. It can kill others.

Jealousy and envy need to be addressed early on if you see red flags and warnings in a partner. They are like a slow-growing, progressive disease. Some people experience feelings of mild envy and jealousy caused by past traumas, heartbreaks and experiences that led them to build strong emotional fortresses for self-protection. Others, however, are a bit more disturbed and you will need to pay attention to your intuition and get away from anyone (friend or romantic partner) that is severely and possibly pathologically jealous. Jealousy in its ultimate form has been the root cause of numerous murders, suicides and other tragedies. If you see these early warning signs, please seek help and prepare to re-evaluate your connection to this person.

Red Flags are important to the Urban Goddess. She is aware that there are often warning bells as well as subtle signs that can often alert her that troubled waters may lie ahead. She pays attention when she feels that something may be "off." She observes, listens, asks questions!

Red Flags and Warnings:

Goddess Pearls of Wisdom ...
"You are placed a pedestal early on. It may feel great to be treated very special, but if, over time, your partner expects you to remain perfect, this is a warning sign of an unhealthy relationship."

- When your human side emerges, the dangerous controller/jealous partner will be disappointed, frustrated and angry with you, especially if you voice your opinions or disagree with them. They will manipulate you, punish you, and diminish your self-worth in order to get you to comply with their agenda.

- The dangerous controller and jealous partner will often play the role of victim. They will try to guilt you into feeling sorry for them and when they have hurt you or wronged you, they will NOT take any responsibility. Problems are always all your fault.

- Gaslighting. This is a situation where someone tries to manipulate your perceptions. One example is someone who seems to always change their story even when you know they told you something different on another occasion. It may help to journal and/or document things. When you're with this type of person, you can feel as if you are losing your mind. Gaslighters also are often pathological liars.

ɬ Pay attention. Address mild jealous reactions, both in yourself and your partner immediately. Do not be afraid to address these issues. You must call each other out on it in a gentle but firm way and communicate your feelings. They will fester if you do not. Do not let jealousy — in you or your partner — get out of control.

ɬ Take some responsibility. Become aware of your own triggers of envy and jealousy. They have no place in a confident goddess's life. You can begin eliminating that ugly green monster by practicing positive affirmations and self-care. Communicate your needs and feelings.

ɬ Trust your judgment. This cannot be stressed often enough. Do not remain in a relationship that is becoming dangerous to you. Seek help. Life is too short to remain in a constant state of fear or distress.

Chapter Eight
The Urban Goddess on Loss, Courage and Uncertainty

"We gain strength, courage and confidence by each experience in which we really stop to look fear in the face.... we must do that which we think we cannot."
~ Eleanor Roosevelt

Sometimes life goes along smoothly. Days or weeks may go by (even months) without much of a hitch or change. Then like a bolt of lightning, something happens and the world as we once knew it is somehow different. The question becomes, how did I get here and what do I do now?

Life-changing events can come in many forms, whether it is a health scare, car accident, illness of a loved one, job loss, financial difficulty, divorce, breakup, a move, the loss of your pet, or a betrayal. These difficult events will often cause grief and disappointment.

No matter how rough the road, the Urban Goddess knows instinctively, deep down, that she will get through it. She may not be sure how things will work out, but she is certain it somehow will. She keeps the faith.

You see, in the end, it is all about how you choose to handle challenges that come your way.

Sorrow and grief are natural, normal reactions to loss and change. But that sorrow will eventually lessen over time.

What we choose to do with our thoughts, our feelings and ourselves as we slowly improve is what defines us best.

Many people who have experienced great loss and heartbreak ultimately gain enormous strength after loss. It doesn't happen overnight — it takes time. But those people will often tell you they began a new journey on the other side of loss and heartbreak. For example, many people who have lost loved ones give of their time and volunteer, spearhead supportive groups, and help others when they are in need.

No matter how difficult the loss or change for you, there is a light if you seek it. There is always support.

Breakups

"Relationships are like glass: sometimes it's better to leave them broken then to try to hurt yourself putting them back together." ~ Unknown

Breaking up is hard to do. I can't live without you, I can't breathe without you.

Breakups often feel like this in the early stages. Sometimes our relationships end naturally. Although they may have brought meaning, joy, comfort, friendship, or even sex, for a period, some relationships simply run a course or a season, and it's time for the partners to move on.

Yet there are others that don't end with a flow but more of a bang, where the breakup is long and drawn out, filled with lots of drama.

Perhaps you and your partner have grown apart, or have differences so irreconcilable that no matter how hard you try, you will never be compatible.

The transition through the end of a relationship is always uncomfortable, and sometimes painful. Maybe you've been nagged by a sense of unhappiness for a while. Perhaps, though you feel a bit sad or guilty, you met someone else (or heaven forbid your partner did) that seems a better match. Sometimes things change and sometimes things can be mended. But sometimes they can't. This is where jealousy can kick in, even if the relationship isn't right for you any longer. It is natural to feel discomfort when someone you were very close to, who made you feel special, is now making someone else feel special — or at the least isn't into your specialness any longer.

Challenges and fear of loss can make some relationships stronger. Other times it can break the bond permanently. The loss of a relationship can happen at any time — in the early stages of dating, or even many years later, after being married for decades.

All relationships have meaning; some have deeper meaning to us than others. The reasons for a breakup do not really matter, for in the end they are a part of life. Chances are, you will go through at least one breakup in your life, so it's a really good idea to know how to handle them.

Whether your break is a permanent one or a temporary separation it is important to take especially good care of yourself during this time.

Do not neglect yourself, your home, your work, and your children. This is a time to cry, feel sorry for yourself, and then get up and be resilient. Trust in the process that all will work out for the best even though it does not feel like it in the moment.

Take the time to mourn and grieve, within reason. If you feel angry, take up a sport, kick boxing class, running — anything to help you decompress your stress and hurt.

If you have children, do not be afraid or fearful of letting them see you cry. You are human and it shows them that they can be strong and yet be okay with expressing your emotions. Set an example.

During this transition it is very helpful to seek support, encouragement and help from others. A trusted mentor, professional counselor or spiritual advisor would be a good choice. Friends are well-meaning but a professional trained in working with relationship issues can be very supportive and invaluable during this time.

Divorce and Separation

Google the word *divorce* and you will come up with more than 38,000,000 hits. Statistics show that fifty percent of all first marriages end in divorce and sixty percent of second marriages. No one sets out to get divorced after saying "I do" but it happens. You are not alone.

Divorce is never easy. It is never simple. It is always unique in certain ways and it will change you. Sometimes for the better, sometimes for the worse. That part is up to you.

I speak from experience and from working with hundreds of clients during this transitional time. Time does heal most wounds. It really is possible, even likely, that when you heal yourself, learn your lessons, take responsibility and move forward, you will thrive again.

If you and your spouse decide to end your marriage there are nine ways that, while difficult, can make the transition smoother and keep both of you relatively calm through the process. Keep in mind that millions of people divorce so if others could get through that crucible of fire, so can you.

⤸ Don't be a victim, no matter how tempting. It is normal and natural to feel loss, sadness, disappointment, or even great relief but don't act as if you are the only person in the world going through this. You alone are responsible for your actions and reactions.

༄ Don't use the children (young or older) as pawns. They have absolutely nothing to do with your divorce. You can, and will be, loving parents (both of you) for the rest of their lives. Grow up and set an example.

༄ Maintain self-care daily. Millions of people divorce and thrive. It may take you a while to get on your feet and it may feel like the end of the world for some. That too shall pass.

༄ Allow yourself to grieve. Do not hesitate to reach out to someone to talk to. You will need to talk and you need people around you who are good listeners.

༄ Take things one day at a time.

༄ Do not feel ashamed if you feel depressed or hopeless. Immediately seek professional help.

༄ Limit the drama. Do something worthwhile and rewarding with your frustration, hurt, and anger. Learn to turn it around. Expend your energy in constructive ways. Be of service. No matter how difficult and challenging divorce is, there is always someone who needs more help than you. You will truly be amazed how this will help heal you.

༄ Always remember that it really is possible, even likely, that you and your ex can be friends when the time is right.

༄ Always take the high road. Nothing lasts forever. Perhaps this union no longer served you or your spouse's higher good and it was time to move on. Easier said than done, but not impossible.

~Section Three~

The Urban Goddess Lesson on Heroes and Heartbreakers

Heartbreakers come in all shapes and sizes. Unfortunately, there isn't a neon sign on their forehead. Heroes also come in all shapes and sizes. They too come without a label. In the beginning, it is difficult to tell the difference. Good guys and lethal lovers will give off some of the same signals. Over time, the good guy remains good, and the bad boy, well…

The only way you can, as the amazing Urban Goddess you are, figure out the difference is to pay attention, look for consistency, and OBSERVE!

Chapter Nine

The Urban Goddess and the Hero

"We are all ready to be savage in some cause. The difference between a good man and a bad one is the choice of the cause."
~ William James

A man who has hero characteristics is almost always going to be a good, loving partner. A hero will be more understanding, supportive, emotionally together, empathic, low on selfishness and high on selflessness.

Of course not all selfish people are heartbreakers and not all selfless people are heroes. Having said that, it is important to take note that in general, selfless people (unless they are very co-dependent and emotionally imbalanced) are going to be confident, balanced and compassionate.

Selfish people, on the other hand (whether they fall under the Heartbreaker category or not), will tend to become rather frustrating and disappointing to deal with over time. They have an imbalanced sense of entitlement and haughtiness. They are going to fall short (often very short) on the empathy scale.

It cannot be stated enough how important it is to look for the capacity of empathy in others. A man who is capable of true empathy will not only be a good partner and provider, but will make a wonderful father to your children.

What heroes look for in a relationship

The media, particularly women's lifestyle magazines, promote how important it is to know what you want in a man and relationship.

This is vital to your success in your search. It is also just as important to know some of the key factors that men look for in a woman when searching for a relationship (not a booty call or hookup).

Men have relationships needs and wants too. After coaching many men through the years, I can confidently say that these are some of the traits and characteristics men — including your hero — look for:

- **Acceptance**. A man wants to be loved for who he is. He does not want a woman to try to change him, but he is open to being inspired by her to make some positive changes to his life when he is ready. If you get him and he feels understood by you, believe you have found the magic that will keep the fires burning. This is often why there are so many "emotional affairs" going on. Yes, men love sex and are attracted to physical beauty, but a woman who understands him stands out from the crowd.

- **Communication**. This may seem like a no-brainer but a lot of couples do not communicate about important things, including disagreements. Communication is vital to any relationship but the style in which you choose to communicate (mirroring what you hear each other say, reflective listening, speaking your mind calmly, working on a compromise) are extremely necessary to a good relationship.

- **Great sex.** Let's face it, great sex is really important to a romantic relationship/marriage. Keep it spicy and exciting by looking good and feeling good. Be the woman that attracted him in the beginning.

- **Admiration and respect.** If he is your man and he is a hero to you, show him often how you admire, adore and respect him. Be grateful for gifts you receive from being in each other's lives. It doesn't mean things will be perfect all the time or that you should go around complimenting him 24/7, but be mindful of showing him how special he is. Frankly, if you don't, someone else will and he will be drawn to that.

- **A healthy woman.** Be the woman he fell in love with. Continue to take care of yourself, have interests of your own, work out, and spend time making yourself look and feel good. Many men will say that their girlfriends or wives changed over the years by letting themselves go, emotionally, intellectually and physically. Don't let that be you!

- **Trust.** It is a big leap of faith because we can't be with someone every minute of the day, but men want you to trust them. You don't need to police him, become a drama queen driven by jealousy or envy, or play victim. You need time together and time apart. There should be a healthy balance and no, he does not need to report to you every second, nor should you constantly report in to him. He wants you to know he is with you because he wants to be with you. If you are having difficulty with trust issues, it may be a good idea to talk with someone.

Consider that if you want a man for the long haul, you need to let him be! Let him be your hero and you will reap the rewards.

Why Men Love Women with a Sense of Confidence

An emotionally healthy, strong, confident man loves a woman who exudes confidence. A woman who keeps him on his toes and feels good about herself. She also isn't keeping score. She is a woman who wants to enhance her man's happiness but also believes she deserves and wants her man to keep her happy as well.

Both heroes and heartbreakers will often be attracted to a woman of confidence. The hero will be proud of his woman and will emotionally support her to be all she can be. The heartbreaker will pretend to feel proud of her for a period of time, but before long, she will notice that this lethal lover will be in direct competition with her. He will become critical of her, causing drama and make her feel as if she is stealing the spotlight. He will feel threatened by her achievements and any passion for life that she may have outside of the relationship.

Let me give you advance warning of one particular heartbreaker to watch out for: the narcissist. Narcissists have great difficulty with anyone they perceive as "more in" getting more attention, being held in higher regard even for only a few moments. Their fragile self-esteem and sense of self is rather shaky. (Be sure to read about how to communicate and deal with narcissists. Refer to chapter 16.)

Be confident and reap the rewards.

Heroes and Diamonds in the Rough

Bad boys can be very charming, very sexy, very hot, and often superficially nice. Lots of fun. But they are temporary diversions. They often are players. They often cheat and betray. They often don't want a commitment or a girlfriend or a wife. They often just want to have fun. That's okay if you just want to have fun, but beware.

These bad boys are often highly sexual and experienced, yet quite manipulative and you can get hooked and addicted. The fun will turn to heartbreak if you fall in love.

Some good men (heroes, generally speaking) can go bad temporarily or permanently. Most good men are good most of the time. This is what you are looking for if you have decided you want a healthy relationship. Look for the diamonds in the rough.

Heroes tend to have a strong capacity to be concerned about others and the world around them. They may have average looks, they may tend to be more subtly attractive and classically understated, but their outstanding character and compassion outshines the most handsome of men.

They are often confident, compassionate people who don't have a need or drive to cause harm to others.

They can be very "strong" and "alpha" but have a soft heart.

Heroes have strong empathy for others.

Chapter Ten

The Urban Goddess Knows a Hero When She Sees One

"Life is not measured by the number of breaths we take, but the moments that take our breath away."
~ Maya Angelou

When my beloved father passed away several years ago, the wake and funeral were a bit of a blur. The one thing I do remember vividly is that everyone who knew my father expressed the following sentiment: "Your father was an especially good man."

My dad had many great traits and did some awesome things in his life. Aside from being a great dad, he was a veteran, an artist, musician, and a former government agent. He dealt with many people in his lifetime but made the time and effort to make every one of them feel heard and special. He was always a hero in my eyes, but once he was gone I realized he was a hero to many. There are special qualities that all heroes have in common.

So how does the Urban Goddess recognize a hero?

⤷ He adds value to her life.

⤷ He respects himself and others.

⤷ He has interests of his own but wants, and is committed to, a relationship that is loving and passionate.

⤷ He cares about people, pets, the planet. He also cares about what his special someone cares about.

⤷ He inspires her and encourages her.

⤷ He can communicate (about anything).

⤷ He has worked on himself. He is introspective and emotionally intelligent.

⤷ He seeks a higher level of consciousness.

⤷ He has the capacity for empathy, to feel emotions and not be fearful of expressing them.

⤷ He is genuine, authentic, and smart.

⤷ He is a protector.

⤷ He is successful and enjoys his work.

⤷ He is hot and sexy; the chemistry is thick and he's great in bed!

Chapter Eleven
The Urban Goddess Values Good Communication

"Communication leads to community, that is, to understanding, intimacy and mutual valuing." ~ Rollo May

Communication is vital to any healthy relationship. A healthy balance of conversation is important and necessary to feel validated and important, and the same goes for the other person whether they are a romantic partner, friend, child, family member, colleague or neighbor.

Many people believe they are great communicators but all too often in my office (especially with couples counseling) I see people "talk at" each other, raise their voices, say unkind things and never really "hear" the other person speak.

I strongly suggest you learn and practice good communication skills. Read books, attend seminars, watch videos, do more public speaking, join groups and share thoughts and ideas. Practice with your family, partner, and friends.

Great communication skills are learned behavior and will help you live a more extraordinary life.

Simple communication skills that work:

- Talk to and not at each other.

- Make quiet time to talk.

- Think about what you need to address. Keep it to the point.

- Mirror each other's words before responding and use active listening techniques. This really works! It helps each person feel understood and important.

- Experts will tell you that sometimes a drive in the car or sitting next to each versus opposite each other is better to have a meaningful conversation or to solve a disagreement. It makes each person more relaxed regarding their body language and eye contact.

Chapter Twelve
The Urban Goddess on Sincerity

"I am very picky with whom I give my energy to. I prefer to reserve my time, intensity and spirit exclusively to those who reflect sincerity."
~Dau Voire

Sincerity and trust go hand and hand. We may not always love the truth. We may not want to always see the truth or tell the truth but in the end, as they say, the truth shall set you free.

If we value truth and sincerity within ourselves (and only you can make that clear, personal choice) then it will be very important to you to choose a friend, lover, partner or spouse who also values sincerity.

If you speak your truth, if you expect others to speak their truths, then it will be important to you to surround yourself with like-minded people. Someone who is sincere and trustworthy will have your best interest at heart. They are people who are safe. You can be yourself with them.

Of course, not all people are sincere, and some pretend to be. Many controlling, manipulative, pathological people will act sincere because they have a motive. Wise habits can help you estimate the truthfulness or sincerity of others, such as: paying attention to body language, tone of voice, patterns of behavior, and responses to conflict, challenges or difficulties (both theirs and yours). The best indicators of sincerity are time and consistency.

We all manage many different relationships, whether they're personal (romantic relationships, friendships) or practical (doctors, dentists, contractors, nannies). Whatever the relationship, it should be based on trust and sincerity. It is imperative for emotional health and safety that you only connect with people who are trustworthy and reliable. Everyone has a difficult day. Everyone has a bad mood from time to time. We are human. Seek out people who do as they say, and say as they do. Genuine trust and sincerity will stand the test of time.

Seven Ways to Test Trustworthiness

Ask yourself the following questions.

1. Is your romantic partner emotionally supportive of you and genuinely happy about your accomplishments?

Insincere people are often very competitive with friends and romantic partners. They are envious and jealous deep down. Also pay attention to facial expressions when you tell them something positive regarding yourself. They may tell you they are happy for you but their body language and facial expressions will reveal their true feelings.

2. Does your romantic partner genuinely smile?

The eyes are the windows to the soul. A genuine smile is unmistakable. It's one in which the eyes are actually smiling along with their lips. Their eyes crinkle, the smile is very wide.

3. Is most of what you talk about and do all about them?

If your partner rarely, if ever, considers your schedule, your likes/dislikes, your interests, pay attention. You may not only be dealing with someone who is insincere but someone who is enormously self-absorbed!

4. Does your partner seem too eager?

Just because your partner (or dating partner) asks to see you often in the beginning, it doesn't always mean they believe you could be the love of their life. They may have other motives and only time will reveal those. Many men have been known to see a women often in the very beginning (and call/ text her often) in order to convey a false sense of security and interest just to bed her. Slow and steady wins the race. If he doesn't stick around when you want to pace yourself, let him go!

5. Is it a struggle (or do you have a nagging feeling) that commitment and fidelity are an issue for your partner?

It is very important before committing and being monogamous with your partner that you discuss the facts that are important to you in a relationship. Be clear and honest. Safety, both emotionally and physically, should **always** be a priority in your life!

Sex is fantastic with the right person. That is why it is so IMPORTANT to always discuss needs, wants, boundaries, safety, and health BEFORE you take your clothes off!!

6. Does your partner communicate well?

Honest, sincere people get right to the point. They answer questions and answer them quickly, to the point (directly) and are short-winded. Dishonest answers, lies and untrustworthy responses are often spoken after a longer pause, a deeper breath, a turning away of the eyes or face, a partial covering of the mouth (with a hand or finger). Another tell-tale sign is avoiding the question altogether, spinning the topic away or addressing the topic with a long-winded answer. These aren't always foolproof but many body language experts will tell you these are some of the more common signs of insincerity.

7. Do you trust your perceptions?

If you really want to give someone the benefit of the doubt but are nagged by a suspicion that something feels off, begin to journal your communication. Jot down some of your questions and their answers. Then down the road, ask some of the same questions (at a later date of course) to see if their answers are basically the same. If the story keeps changing, no matter how much you may want to believe this person, you are probably dealing with an insincere liar.

It is never, ever, easy to fall out of love with someone but to remain in love with an insincere, lying partner is giving yourself permission to be hurt over and over again. All people from all walks of life have told a fib here and there. That does not make them dangerous or pathological. A consistently insincere, lying person is pathological and very dangerous to your emotional and physical health. No one can force you to leave such a relationship (and perhaps you can get them into therapy if they are open to that) but if not, it's best to cut your losses.

Chapter Thirteen

The Urban Goddess and the Heartbreaker

"By all means marry. If you get a good partner you'll become happy; if you get a bad one, you'll become a philosopher." ~ Socrates

The wise Urban Goddess will avoid the heartbreaker. So as you stock your emotional beauty toolbox, you'll learn how to recognize a heartbreaker and avoid him.

A heartbreaker is:

- A person who is very attractive but who is irresponsible in emotional relationships.

- A story or event that causes overwhelming distress.

Heartbreakers create a fantasy of a dream come true. They can create tremendous excitement and romance, albeit temporarily. They eventually create drama, chaos, frustration, control, dominance and danger in relationships. Great sex and an affair to remember is their agenda.

Heartbreakers almost always send up red flags, which can be subtle or intense. **Red flags are signs, warnings.** Your intuition kicks in and warns you that something is wrong, off, and dangerous. Unfortunately, heartbreakers leave a lot of destruction in their wake.

In order to protect yourself from a potential heartbreaker, trust your gift of intuition, because the heartbreaker red flags are usually subtle. Think of a relationship with a heartbreaker like a game of chess — deliberate, small moves used by partners who are manipulators and gaslighters who win by carefully planned moves.

Red flags in a relationship are no laughing matter. Though this most often happens in romantic relationships, they can arise in family or work-related dynamics as well.

People who cause you to doubt your perceptions often possess pathological tendencies. There is no cure for pathology and it runs on a spectrum. The truth is, any type of pathology can be dangerous to your health.

Heartbreakers run on a spectrum from mild to severe. Some are selfish. Others manipulative. There are many garden variety types.

Some will go to extremes including creating crazy making behavior. The saying if you play with fire you are going to get burned…..point in case.

When you feel deeply something is off, it is! Don't bury your head in the sand. If you often feel like you are walking on eggshells, being talked down to or treated disrespectfully, it's important to speak up! If your partner seems to be temporarily appeasing you or pays your request no attention, you know where you stand. If he doesn't respect your needs, wishes and desires and isn't willing to at least compromise on important issues to you, there is NO relationship. There is a dictatorship!

Narcissists, sociopaths, and players are often very manipulative and controlling. Abusers also show these traits. Abuse is never just a slap or push. It often begins subtly and slowly. Emotional and verbal abuse grow over time. It can be covert or overt. Abuse can sometimes slip in the back door. It affects all cultures, races, sexual orientations. Abuse destroys lives and murders your soul. It is your responsibility to learn about the warning signs of abuse. Reach out for help, get out and get away.

Note: Sometimes no matter how psychologically swank we may strive to be, toxic people and character disordered people slip their way into our lives. Do not beat yourself up!

It happens. The first time, you get a pass. If it happens a second time, take responsibility and take yourself out of harm's way. Work on the reasons that got you here again. It is the only way out. You may not have asked to be a victim but do not remain one.

There is always help and there are choices.

Heartbreaker Red Flags

Red flags will appear if you know what to look for. Machiavellian manipulators know just how to psychologically control you over time. If they are very high-functioning psychopaths, they will know how to turn on the charm or apologize when needed or confronted.

Good men may do some bad things but they don't deliberately hurt you or try to control. **Love does not equal abuse.**

So here are some examples of dangerous red flags. No one can force you to not get involved or leave a relationship that is dangerous, but red flags will wake you up from your sleeping beauty sleep. If you see these signs, it is best for your emotional health to cut and run. If you decide to stay, you are in for it and placing yourself in harm's way. It doesn't get better.

Universal Red Flags of Heartbreakers

Love Bombing: In the beginning, you will be the recipient of love-bombing. The heartbreaker will do everything in his power to get you to let your guard down and become his. Calls, dates, romance, cards, emails — you name it, he'll do it to sweep you off your feet. You will be told you are the best thing that ever happened to him. He will be whatever you need him to be. No one else understands him. You make him happy. But what you don't know yet is that he wants to own you and control you. Darkness lurks around the corner. You will soon be a fly in the ointment.

Devaluation: As time goes on, after the honeymoon begins to fade a bit, you will begin to see, hear and experience things that will make you question if something is off. It could be boundary violations; for example, you told him something that hurts you and he continues to do the very thing you told him hurts you. He seems to "test" your love and attention. Will you always pick up the phone when he calls? If not, you may be slightly punished. You call him back because you were truly busy and he lets your call go to voicemail. He may give you the silent treatment to punish you. At first you will rationalize and brush it away but over time you will see it is a pattern. Pay attention and observe! He wants your full attention and adoration.

Silent Treatment and hot and cold behavior (inconsistency and intermittent reinforcement). This is a common tactic of heartbreakers. The more they pull back, the more some women want them and they believe their value goes up. Urban Goddesses know better than to get pulled into this cat and mouse game.

Bottom line, if you want some temporary fun and excitement then a heartbreaker may not break your heart. If you are looking for a committed relationship with a loving, caring man who has your best interest at heart, BEWARE and use your smart heart.

Look, listen and observe the signs of a heartbreaker. If you get involved with one, it's best for you to cut your losses and learn your Urban Goddess lesson.

Chapter Fourteen

The Urban Goddess Knows
Men are Transparent

"Women love us for our defects. If we have enough of them, they will forgive us everything, even our gigantic intellects." ~ Oscar Wilde

Most men love women. Most women love men. If you ask most women they would tell you that though they love their children, their jobs, their homes, their friends or hobbies, that a great deal of time is spent talking about and figuring out the men in their lives!

Why are women always trying to figure out men? And why are men often trying to figure out women? Because, as author John Gray says, *men are from Mars and women are from Venus.* Then again, we aren't really all that different in many ways, but enough to make us curious and sometimes challenging to figure out!

A simple but important Urban Goddess lesson is that most men (if not all men) are really pretty simple to figure out. They can be a king, an oil tycoon, a superior athlete, president of a corporation or the FedEx guy, but bottom line is it doesn't matter where he is from or what he does for a living, he thinks very similarly to his brothers.

Goddess Pearls of Wisdom ...
"If you listen, a man will tell you everything you need to know about himself." ~ A Wise Woman

With the exception of a sociopathic personality (what you see is definitely NOT what you get) most men will tell you who they are pretty quickly and simply.

A man will tell you everything you need to know about him and the way he feels about you through his actions.

Now this is not to suggest that you shouldn't listen to what a man says. He says a lot of important things. (Okay, maybe at times not so important to you, but could be important to him!)

Also, if he loves you he will tell you. So words are important. Who doesn't love hearing that they look beautiful and are adored?

This goddess advice is meant to help you understand that over-thinking situations and grilling your partner is a bad strategy.

A great deal of the time, what you see and observe is what is really happening. Talk to him, communicate with him and listen.

Let's get real. You know if your man loves you or not, if he is cheating or not, if he is in it for the long haul or not. You may not know one hundred percent, but you have a pretty good inclination.

Be sure your man does not abuse you in any way. Heroes never raise a hand to their woman — or any woman. Abusers often do. **Always leave if you are being abused**. It only gets worse.

Chapter Fifteen
The Urban Goddess on Relationship Games

"Well-being cannot exist just in your own head. Well-being is a combination of feeling good as well as actually having meaning, good relationships and accomplishment." ~Martin Seligman

There is rarely a relationship that doesn't have some form of a "game" attached to it, at least in the beginning. Both healthy and unhealthy relationships begin with "tests" of the future beloved.

This behavior is normal and natural, and can actually be exciting and adrenaline-pumping.

Having said that, there is a fine line where the "games" can become manipulative and downright cruel and abusive. The Goddess learns to know the difference and acts accordingly.

There comes a point where two mature individuals will cease the testing games and focus on the relationship. The fun never has to stop but the games do if they are no longer serving the good of the relationship.

Sometimes mind games become the glue that keep certain relationships together and in turn cause a great deal of drama, anxiety, angst and an addiction to the highs and lows. We see this often on reality television shows. These relationships may thrive on that type of excitement, but over time become very toxic and dangerous to those involved.

Keep in mind that when mind games go beyond flirty fun, they are being used often because your partner is unable to confront you directly about something that is bothering them.

If you see this, confront them gently but do not let it slide. Being assertive can momentarily soften the insecurity or lack of confidence. Tell them to cut it out. Enough already. If they don't comply at first, tell them you will speak to them again when they can do so in an adult manner. (You can add some humor but stick to your guns.)

Most times this will help within the realm of an overall healthy partner and relationship. Keep in mind if your partner continues to do hurtful things, say hurtful things, disrespect your opinions and boundaries, you could be dealing with an emotional abuser, narcissist or sociopath.

Chapter Sixteen
The Urban Goddess and the Narcissist

"The brick walls are not there to keep us out. The brick walls are there to give us a chance to show how badly we want something….the brick walls are there to stop the people who don't want it badly enough."
~ Randy Pausch

Narcissism runs on a spectrum from mild to pathological. It is not difficult to fall in love with a narcissist. Often the reason is because, in the beginning, the narcissist is so lovable, vulnerable, adorable, caring, considerate, humorous, generous, attentive, and adoring. We become their happiness.

So, what if an Urban Goddess falls for a narcissist?

If the narcissist in her life turns out to be mildly to moderately self-absorbed, it won't be easy, but she can learn to compromise, adjust, and improve her boundaries to live a reasonably comfortable life with him—though it will never be a bed of roses.

If she ever realizes she has fallen in love with a pathological narcissist, she is in for it. One of the biggest red flags goes up soon after the honeymoon idealization phase is over: She is kicked off of her pedestal and treated with great disdain, engaged in psychological warfare, and devalued. The tricky part is that she will be the recipient of hot and cold behavior; the old slot machine theory. She will continue to keep playing for the jackpot because the small wins entice her to keep gambling on the big payoff. She becomes addicted to the rush of the reward, so she hangs on just a *little* longer. Like the proverbial carrot on a string.

Oftentimes, she becomes addicted to the narcissist. The narcissist also becomes addicted to her, but for very different reasons. Through learned behavior, she comes to believe that he is god-like. He leads her down the garden path to believe she is very special to him. But over time, she realizes the huge emotional price to be paid in exchange for that special status. The more she desires the attention of the narcissist, the more he will pull away. When she pulls back, he often comes after her. This is a common but dangerous dance that narcissists and their lovers play.

When he is displeased with her for even the most innocent of slights, he will punish her with his cold silence by withdrawing affection, sex, his company, even his voice. The relationship becomes a dangerous liaison in which she can truly lose her sense of self. He wants to own her — literally possess her — and she is soon swept away. Within a short time he will often reward her again when she defers to his wishes. The pathological narcissist is similar to the Greek god Zeus, who is the center of his universe and everyone else is but a mere satellite orbiting around him.

Narcissists must have their way. They *need* to be in control, they *need* to win. In today's world, our society is filled with narcissists, an issue the media claims may be one of the personality disorder epidemics of our time.

It is important to learn about narcissism and how to handle a narcissist in your life. Why? Because there are so many of them, and even a narcissist in the mildest form can wreak havoc on your life.

Not all narcissists are not beyond help. Having said this, it is important to remember that living with and loving a narcissist over any length of time is **NOT** for most people. Unless the narcissist wants to change and learn healthier ways of coping, there is little anyone else can do.

The following is a list of some constructive ways to deal with a narcissist with possibilities.

Choose your battles wisely. Don't fear calling him out on issues that have led him to cross or intrude upon your boundaries. In order to have a meaningful relationship with a narcissist, you must gain and keep his respect. Don't be a doormat with a narcissist.

They are very easily slighted and ultra-sensitive to being perceived as less than or wrong — this will cause immediate humiliation and insecurity. Be aware of this, and speak directly and calmly when discussing issues. Do not blame, but speak in "I" statements. I feel, I need, I am.

Build a tough skin. The narcissist will often be sarcastic, ambivalent, and critical, but then loving and attentive. You will need to have a strong sense of yourself and not take everything personally. This will take practice, but learn to control your automatic defenses — they only escalate the narcissist. Stay as unemotional as possible during confrontations and often your calm response will defuse the situation.

Learn to lower your expectations and strengthen your sense of self. *Narcissists desperately need admiration and adoration.* They are a drug to him, which means that even though you may be viewed as very special to him (in the beginning and intermittently) he will always need more than one person can offer. He often needs a fan club. He will have an insatiable need to be the best and the brightest, so you may often take a back seat. If you want to remain important to a narcissist, do not depend on him to give you consistent emotional support, love, caring, communication, and companionship. You must accept him for who he is. Most narcissists will never change. Using this approach, you will learn to cope more effectively with the challenges of a relationship with someone who is difficult and self-absorbed.

Feed his ego, within reason. There is no way around it: If you want to remain with a narcissist and keep the peace (and even help him become more aware of your presence and needs), you will need to compliment him often…but it must be *sincere*. Speak from your heart, and be genuine. Tell him the things you truly love and admire about him, and tell him often. Many men (not just narcissists) need admiration and a reminder that they are important to that special someone in their lives. The love of a good woman (and a sexy one) is very important to a man. This may sound a bit old-fashioned, but it still holds true today. You need to voice it and show him regularly.

Take care of yourself (physically and emotionally). This is important for your self-esteem, important for your man, and shows the world you respect your-self.

In order to live comfortably with a narcissist you will need to learn to accept limitations. At times your relationship will be a roller coaster, at others times perhaps the best relationship you have ever had. You — and **only** you — will need to weigh your options and make a decision as to whether you are living your best life. Be honest with yourself. If a fully engaged physical, emotional, and spiritual relationship that is reciprocal in nature is what you seek, then you may find a relationship with a narcissist to be very heartbreaking.

Always remember to never, ever remain in a relationship that is becoming, or has become, abusive in any way. If you believe you are being abused, please seek immediate help.

Chapter Seventeen
The Urban Goddess and the Sociopath

"No one can make you feel inferior without your consent."
~ Eleanor Roosevelt

D
r. Susan Forward, in her enlightening, bestselling book, *When Your Lover Is a Liar,* shares that if there is one man you *must* leave, it is the sociopath.

Sociopathy runs on a spectrum, as do many of the character and personality disorders. Though we won't delve into much empirical research here, it is important that you educate yourself about the sociopathic character disturbance of relating.

Why? Well there are many reasons, but out of all of the lethal lovers and heartbreakers, the sociopath, along with the pathological version of the narcissist, is an emotional predator.

It can be very destructive and hurtful to be in a relationship with one because they really do have a missing emotional chip. It's just not there, or if it is it is very lacking.

Therapist Sandra Brown, in her book *How to Spot a Dangerous Man,* says that personality disorders are permanent disorders.

So what does that mean for you?

It means that if you are dating one, it would be in your best interest to find out all you can about this potential partner. It means that if you come to find out that this person has a personality disorder (especially from the Cluster B group in the DSM, the *Diagnostic Statistical Manual of Mental Health Disorders*) you may be better off throwing in the towel early on, as a relationship with this person will be difficult at best and possibly dangerous depending on the severity.

Sociopaths have a severe character disturbance, with some worse than others of course (think Bernie Madoff, Scott Peterson). But practically all of them will wreak havoc on your life.

They lack empathy and they lack a conscience, therefore they can't walk in the shoes of someone — anyone — who has emotions and feelings. Scientific research seems to show there is a region of the brain (frontal lobe) and a specific area called the amygdala that is compromised, or non-functioning in people that may be sociopaths or borderline sociopaths. If you would like to do further study on this, Dr. Robert Hare is an excellent source on this topic.

Writer Donna Anderson has an excellent website, Lovefraud.com, with videos, reading materials and a blog that will be very insightful for you to check out if you suspect you are dealing with a sociopath.

Let's cover some red flags you can look for if you think you may be with one.

Though many, many men who are not sociopathic can be charming and charismatic, the sociopath seems too over-the-top charming. Many people, over time, report that the sociopathic style personality seems to have "fakeness" to it.

Sociopaths don't always have a type that they target. They seem to just as easily take on victims who are beautiful as well as those who are very average-looking.

They are very smart, very opportunistic and usually want something from you. It could be sex, status, a promotion, your connections; it could be your money, your home, your investments, or he may just want someone as arm candy to boost his ego.

The sociopath often plays mind games and gives intermittent reinforcement. You will never know if you are coming or going with them.

You will often walk on eggshells, be gaslighted by them and never feel quite sure where you stand.

They can be very loving at times, especially in the early stages of a relationship or near a possible ending. I encourage you to read about love-bombing.

They can turn on you in an instant. Hot and cold behavior is common.

Do pay attention to your intuition. Many people who have gotten involved with a sociopath report later that they had a gut feeling early on that something was off. Heed that inner voice.

Chapter Eighteen

The Urban Goddess and the Player

"The man who does not value himself, cannot value anything or anyone." ~ Ayn Rand

Players are not all bad guys and heartbreakers. Some of them are truly just trying to find their "soul mates," learn from experience and eventually become amazing boyfriends, husbands and fathers.

That is *some* of them, of course. Now the other groups of players who continue playing all through their lives are not so adorable. They are Peter Pans in men's clothing and really quite selfish. These are the guys that are on an eternal search. The truth is they have a lot of inner stuff going on and self-medicate with the attention and sex of several women, usually all at the same time.

Perhaps you recognize the player. He is often the guy that never grew up. He is non-committal and likes it that way. If you do too, you are fine entering a relationship with a player.

If you want someone with more relationship substance, well, you'd better start looking elsewhere.

Usually the player is fearful of engulfment, intimacy and commitment. Now some players are just die-hard Don Juans. They are suave, smooth operators who don't miss a beat. They know how to play your heartstrings, they tell you what you want to hear and they will take you to the moon and back.

Really all they want is for you to fall in love with them. Get your attention and then they will be moving on.

Some of these men are rather harmless and you can write them off. A few, though, fall into the sociopathic category and you want to be especially careful with these.

The sociopathic type is a dangerous fellow. He is almost always good looking, very charismatic, financially comfortable and loves to take big risks. He gets a real high from engaging in high-risk behaviors, which could be anything from wrangling alligators to taking huge risks in the stock market. But what sets the sociopath apart from your average thrill seeker is the pleasure he gets from emotionally hurting people, especially women.

If you think you may be with someone who has sociopathic traits, please read the chapter on sociopaths and check out my recommendations for websites and books that will give you more information.

Some players are honest about their juggling or marital status. Others are not. If you get involved with one, you need to learn as many facts about him as you can. This is your life and your heart. Know what you are getting into and make sure you can handle it.

There is another type that is basically a good guy (not a player) who has had an indiscretion or two. He had the experience, it was fun (or maybe it wasn't), it was new, he felt guilty, he got over it, and he doesn't plan on doing it again. For this guy, it sort of kind of just happened and no one was hurt in the process.

So here are some red flag warnings to help you decide if you want to continue seeing a "player" to determine your level of risk. The only conundrum here is that you need to know what you want.

❧ If you are looking for a good time, some fun evenings, good sex and a short-term relationship, then a player may suit you well for a while. One thing is for certain — a player will show you a good time!

❧ If you are looking for a long-term relationship or marriage, a player may not be the best choice for you. Even though you hear stories of players finally finding the one woman of their dreams and forsaking all others, it is a stretch to think this will be your experience. Some of them are capable of this but others may return to form shortly after the wedding. It's a crap shoot. If you fall in love, it is going to hurt when he disappoints you, so if you think he is a player, get out early.

❧ Look for hot/cold, on-again-off-again behavior. Look for consistency. Consistency and keeping his word isn't a guarantee you're not dealing with a player, but most of the time it shows that he has a genuine interest in you and cares about your feelings.

❧ Observe words and actions, and see if they match.

❧ Communicate and pay attention to red flags such as inconsistencies, difficulty reaching him, later nights at the office, his phone vibrating often and he doesn't answer it. There are lots of websites and information available if you want to investigate further.

❧ Tell him your needs and wants. If he is willing to make some sacrifices for you and compromise, there may be some hope. Most true players are very selfish and won't budge.

❧ Always know the difference between someone who talks the talk but doesn't walk the walk. Actions and words need to be consistent, always. If your gut tells you he is lying but he denies it, tell him to cut it out but don't keep policing him. If you love him, it is worth a try, but don't bank on change. You may want to get yourself into therapy to talk this out and make some decisions.

If you think he may be a player, perhaps the best thing to do after you talk with him is to take a break or consider permanently ending things. Leopards don't change their spots. Either he will come around when he is ready (and if you are still available) or he won't. It may greatly disappoint you but you want to be with someone who can make you happy. An Urban Goddess deserves that.

Chapter Nineteen
The Urban Goddess on Ambivalence

"I don't think it's necessarily healthy to go into relationships as a needy person. Better to go in with a full deck." ~Angelica Huston

A wise goddess woman knows that it is important for both her and her partner to have independence and inter-dependence in a relationship. Space and privacy are healthy for oneself as well as a partnership.

You have to believe that you offer your partner something special and unique. You need to feel balanced within yourself to know that some people will ride the journey with you, bumps and all and others will step out the back door hoping to go unnoticed.

Both a hero and heartbreaker in your life may need and want space. Usually the difference is that the hero wants his space to explore and enjoy his life while respecting yours.

The heartbreaker often wants his space to fill that space with bad boy activities.

There is really one simple formula for a man who seems to want an unreasonable amount of space, and that is, give him the galaxy! If you need or want more time, attention and thoughtfulness, and you are certain you are not being unreasonable in your request, then you may be in the wrong relationship for you and you should get out.

Communicate and discuss your needs and thoughts (again within reason, don't over analyze!) then use his response as your guide.

Sometimes women can be their own worst enemy. Some women believe there is something off with a partner or wrong with her if he wants time and space away from her. But a reasonable amount of space is normal and healthy.

You need to discuss with your partner what is reasonable and works for both of you to feel loved and comfortable. If, time and time again, this is an issue you should seek professional guidance.

If you are finding that too many things in your relationship do not align it may be time to throw in the towel. Only you can decide what makes you really happy and you deserve that.

Chapter Twenty
The Urban Goddess Avoids Destructive Relationships

"Sometimes the hardest part of being a great catch is realizing not everyone is strong enough to hold you." ~ Wesley

A destructive relationship is one in which a person (man or woman) is presently (or in the past) causing damage to your spiritual, physical, emotional, mental health and well-being.

Some people have a very high tolerance for abuse and mistreatment due to their past. Others have a very low tolerance. But the healthy person has ZERO tolerance.

Previously, we discussed many universal red flags of abuse or potential abuse. Pay attention to them and do not bury your head in the sand!

Especially listen to your intuition at this time. Even though your partner may not physically harm you, your instincts will tell you if he is emotionally or psychologically abusing you. You will feel uneasiness in your gut. Listen to it.

Abuse often does not begin as a slap, push or a punch. It is often subtle and grows like a disease over time.

Abusers are not all rough and tough men externally. They can be very polished, upstanding citizens in their community. They can be high-powered executives who are snakes in suits.

Abuse often begins in the mind and after a "honeymoon period," abusers tend to subtly begin playing mind and control games which will slowly chip away at your self-esteem and worth. It will happen so slowly and so methodically that you may not notice it for a while.

The abuser does not have your best interest at heart though they claim that they do. Oh and they love you too. But the real motive behind this is that they want you to assuage their fear of abandonment, fear of being alone, low self-worth, mental health issues, or past traumas. Also, with some men abuse can be motivated by gender and cultural differences.

The bottom line is that they want you to feel that no one can love you the way they can. By having power, control and dominance they will one day have you in a position when your self-esteem has plummeted. This is how abuse grows and why so many people find it amazingly difficult to leave an abuser. It is because she so often has become so dependent on him for her self-worth.

Heartbreakers come in all shapes and sizes, all cultures and colors.

Abusers, narcissists, borderline sociopaths, players, controllers, and manipulative people in general, can be very charming and charismatic in the beginning and even for a period of time into a relationship. Eventually, though, your intuition will kick in and you will begin to see the abuser's true colors. Don't remain in any relationship where your partner does not have your best interest at heart. Remember what therapist Sandra Brown says:

"Pathological disorders are permanent disorders."

These abusers are wolves in sheep's clothing. They have an agenda. You are but an extension of them. Very often in these types of relationships you are a means to an end. Read about a personality traits called the "Dark Triad." These toxic people are very dangerous in relationships and in society. Knowledge is power.

Wolves in sheep's clothing will want your friendship, love, advice, company, a shoulder to lean on, love and support (financial, emotional and sexual). Their motives may be as simplistic as boosting their ego, or it could be as disastrous and heinous as wanting to steal your financial fortune, or even your life. I urge you to check out Dr. George Simon's books on this topic — they are very informative.

Even Urban Goddesses can be blindsided or hoodwinked by these charmers. No one is immune at first, even the professionals. That is why when you see the signs early on, RUN.

The Urban Goddess pays attention and uses her smart mind and heart.

If things don't add up, they don't add up! She trusts her judgment.

If she sees or feels abuse, she tailgates out of there.

It is not your job to mend dysfunctional people; leave that to professionals. It is your job to give them a phone number to a great therapist and be on your way.

Chapter Twenty-One
The Urban Goddess Knows a Hero from a Heartbreaker

"In the long run, we shape our lives, and we shape ourselves. The process never ends until we die, and the choices we make our ultimately our own responsibility." ~ Eleanor Roosevelt

Both a hero and heartbreaker in your life may want space, but the difference is that the hero always returns when he begins to miss his "other," and the heartbreaker (and other frogs), well, that is a different story.

Communication, compatibility and timing are as crucial to the success of a relationship as attraction, both emotionally and physically. There are so many "right" and "ripe" ingredients that go into a great relationship that it is a wonder how we ever make them work to begin with, even for a time.

Therapist Rhonda Findling wrote a great book called *The Commitment Cure*. If you find you may be with an ambivalent man, be sure to get this book. It is insightful and very helpful to those dealing with these types of partners.

Here are some questions to ask yourself if you are dealing with hot/cold behavior:

How is this working for me?

Have I communicated my needs to my partner and has he shared his? Have we come to a mutual understanding of how to have our needs met?

Do I often feel secure or anxious in this relationship?

Do I appreciate some free time for each of us to do separate things or do I feel neglected? Am I being reasonable or not?

What feelings of his ambivalence (or mine) are being brought to the surface? How do I feel? (Sad, neglected, taken for granted, etc.)

Is your relationship exciting because it is full of drama? Be aware that drama often masks the real underlying issues that are difficult to talk about.

Do you provoke arguments with each other because you honestly have difficulty being vulnerable and talking about emotional intimacy?

In *The Commitment Cure,* Findling says it is very important to have self-discipline. Being mindful of the drama and refusing to participate in it is very important.

If you are in a relationship with an ambivalent heartbreaker, you will need to get most of your emotional needs met elsewhere. All you can do is make your needs known but be realistic. Only you can decide if you can handle a relationship like this.

Some men do come around, but again, only you can decide if you have enough patience to wait, or if you're willing to take that risk. Those who remain ambivalent often will eventually 1) break up, 2) get married and have affairs, or 3) get divorced. It is difficult to predict.

Professional counseling — individually or as a couple — may be the best solution.

Goddess Pearls of Wisdom on Heroes and Heartbreakers

Psychologist Frank Farley suggests there are a number of factors that distinguish a hero:

- Risk-taking behavior.

- Capacity for compassion, kindness, empathy and altruism.

- Heroes are often ordinary people with a good moral compass that do extraordinary things, even in the simple things of life.

- Look for empathy and compassion.

- Understand what a hero looks for in a woman if you are seeking a healthy relationship.

- Know what you want as well.

Heartbreakers, on the other hand, whether due to childhood issues, family structure, abuse, genetic makeup, or cultural and media influences, usually lack most if not all the hero characteristics. For the long haul, that is. The heartbreaker may certainly attempt to exhibit these in the beginning of a relationship, but they will appear contrived over time.

Chapter Twenty-Two

The Urban Goddess New Old-Fashioned Rules for Dating

"Often romantic relationships fail because you are trying to get someone to fall in love with the YOU that you never discovered."
— Shannon L. Adler

Dating can be fun, exhausting, necessary, interesting, disastrous, boring, exciting (you can fill in the rest). Sometimes you may be very drawn to someone by that wonderful thing we call chemistry and other times you may walk away thinking "no way" and promptly move on.

There isn't any way to predict what person will be the lid to your pot, but there are certain jewels of wisdom that have withstood the test of time:

⚬ Know why you are dating. What is your goal? Is it to have some temporary fun? Are you truly looking for a long-term relationship/ marriage with the right person?

⚬ Be open to meeting all kinds of people. Perhaps your type was always the handsome, rugged fireman but a friend wants to introduce you to a Wall Street stockbroker or an IT brainaic geek type. You still may end up with a fireman, but it is worth it to explore a few of your options before making any final decisions. Many people have fallen in love with people that weren't "their type."

⚬ Ask questions when out on a date. Also, pay attention if your date asks you questions (good) but not too many questions (bad).

It is important that you get to know your date and get some imperative information during a first date. Do you know his last name? Marital status? If divorced or widowed, how long? Where does he live? Work? Enjoy yourself but be smart. Pay attention to body language, and even the way he treats service people. Does he speak with respect? Does he seem anxious? Is he complaining about something already on a first date? Is he mentioning his ex or exes too often? Is life happy for him or is he a big complainer? Does he appear sincere?

Does he appear attracted to you? When he speaks to you does he engage in comfortable eye contact or does he often look away? Does he give you proper attention when you speak or is he ogling every woman that passes by?

- Do not reveal too much information about yourself too early. Some women are "chatty Cathy" types, prone to over-sharing. There is such a thing as TMI—too much information—so keep that in check. With a good guy, this may be fine. With a bad boy (and you don't know this yet) it can be downright dangerous.

- If you enjoy drinking, try not to have any alcohol or limit it to one drink on a first date. You want to be of clear mind.

- Do not hesitate for a moment to leave if you feel uncomfortable or unsafe.

- Feel confident and sassy. If this is someone you would like to see again, be light, breezy and fun on the date. If he feels similarly you will hear from him fairly soon after. If you don't, do not get your hopes up. Most men say if they are interested and attracted to a potential relationship partner, they will call her within three days. It doesn't mean if he calls on the fourth day he doesn't like you but it does mean that if he waits a week (or doesn't call) the Urban Goddess would say NEXT and move on! Men know very quickly whether they feel a spark or not. Also, men usually fall in love early on or not at all. Men can find you attractive and yet not want to date you or have a relationship. Yes, it's complicated sometimes!

- You can glean a great deal of information about someone on a first date. Pay attention to his words, actions, thoughts, conversation. If at the end of the date you think "maybe" then it may be wise to agree to a second date even if he isn't "your type." If your answer is no or probably not, then don't second guess yourself. Don't go out with him again.

꙳ This may seem very old-fashioned to some of you but history has proven that this still works best: **Man pursues woman**. It doesn't mean you can never call or text him but it does mean in the early stages, that if you are interested in a particular man, you let him come to you. He should call you, text you, email you, ask to spend time with you. Once a relationship is established, there can be more give and take.

Let him be the hunter.

꙳ Try your best to be independent and confident even if you fall madly in love with someone. Yes, it is difficult when you are in love and you want to breathe the same air and be close and intimate. He should be free to come and go and so should you. Accountability will come more naturally as time goes on. A little space, mystery and independence can go a long way in keeping both of you interested, excited and in love.

꙳ If you begin to form a relationship with a special someone, live and love passionately but never lose your smarts. Some abusive, controlling, dangerous men (who go above and beyond a little bad boyishness) can be too good to be true and very attentive and loving in the early stages.

Abusiveness should never come as a shock to you. There are always small signs before the big red flags. Pay attention.

If a man is disrespecting you, speak up. If he doesn't change his ways or changes for a short period of time but constantly reverts back to form, let him go. Disrespect breeds contempt and the abuse will increase. Love is not about suffering and cruelty. It should be exciting, wonderful and safe. Exciting and wonderful most of the time (a little bickering and disagreement is common) but it should feel safe one hundred percent of the time. Pay attention to that.

Don't get stuck on someone who isn't interested in you. Learn to always have the strength to leave a relationship if you need to.

~Section Four~

Urban Goddess
Reflections and Takeaways

An Urban Goddess knows that the present moment is all we really have. Everyone gets the same twenty-four hours in a day. What you choose to ultimately do with your time, your thoughts, your mind, your body, and your soul is ultimately up to you. If you want to live with more purpose, more bounce in your step, more balance and joy, consider making the time for reflection, reprogramming, restoring, relaxing and then rebooting. Legendary Katharine Hepburn said it best: "If you obey all the rules, you miss all the fun!"

Chapter Twenty-Three
The Urban Goddess Understands Inner Bliss

"When you are different, sometimes you don't see the millions of people who accept you for what you are. All you notice is the person who doesn't." ~ Jodi Picoult

There are many ways you can improve a romantic relationship or friendship immediately without much effort or overanalyzing. Sometimes something as simple as a hug, a random "thinking of you" text or email, making that extra cup of coffee or remembering something important to someone else can make a positive difference and bring people closer. Simple, well-meaning gestures can often have a big impact on someone. Never underestimate the power of small acts of kindness.

- Revel in your uniqueness. Stand tall and proud. Stop your jealousy and envy now; they have no place in your new confident life.

- Illuminate and radiate your femininity with fearlessness, passion, compassion and confidence.

- Dream big but live mindfully in the simple moments.

- Treat others as you wish to be treated.

- Let go of perfectionism. Honor the imperfection of being human and your own uniqueness.

- Do not force change on others. Inspire, set examples, and focus on changing your thoughts.

- Be smart with your heart, today, tomorrow and always.

- Learn the red flags of destructive people and relationships. Listen to your inner voice.

- Celebrate your life by being grateful each day for all the wonder that surrounds you.

- Learn to let go of labels and judgments. This is not an easy task but you can learn to surrender the outcome.

- Honor your life by living blissfully, boldly, passionately.

- Be true to yourself.

- Speak up.

- Set boundaries and enforce them.

- Empower your inner bitch.

- Have a sense of humor. Don't take life too seriously!

- Learn ways to accept uncertainty and change.

Take the time to enjoy your life. Seek bliss and it will find you.

Chapter Twenty-Four
Ways the Urban Goddess Improves Her Relationships

"This above all: to thine own self be true." ~ *William Shakespeare*

- She takes responsibility for her own happiness.

- She does what she says she's going to do, knowing that builds trust.

- She admits her mistakes. We are all human.

- She's realistic and can push through the hard days.

- She's in or out. She'll either give it her all or let it go.

- She works to be an amazing listener.

- She's affectionate.

- In relationships, she knows each partner must have each other's back.

- She gives her friends and loved ones space.

- She understands the importance of communication.

- She expresses her feelings.

- She encourages those she loves and looks for encouragement in return.

- She forgives. And forgives. And forgives.

- She laughs and smiles often.

- She's passionate and sexy with her partner.

- She fights fair, even if others don't.

- She commits to a date night with her partner.

- She'll always clarify, and won't assume or accuse without cause.

- She loves from her soul.

Chapter Twenty-Five
The Urban Goddess Surrenders and Celebrates Her Fabulousness

"It is better to risk starving to death than surrender. If you give up on your dreams, what's left?" ~ Jim Carrey

To surrender means to let go of the outcome. It does not mean you are giving up or giving in. It is a learned behavior and you will see over time it works.

Surrendering is giving the universe permission to put you on the path you were supposed to be on in the first place! It means letting God, your higher power, nature, the laws of the universe, Mother Nature, help direct you to where you are supposed to be.

Basically it is belief that all will fall into place and everything will work out as it should. Believe and you shall receive.

Often times, perhaps even most times, there really isn't a firm right or wrong about a situation. Many of us see things similarly and yet many more of us see things or interpret things in our own unique ways. Some of life's challenges are not set in stone or black or white but fall more into a gray zone. Understanding that is one thing, but staying stuck in that gray zone is another.

It is important to make decisions. Some of them will lead you to great happiness and satisfaction, others may bring more difficulty than you anticipated, but one thing is for sure—all of them will lead you to growth.

You can read a million books, go to hundreds of seminars but nothing will teach you as well as your life experiences.

This is why as much as we love our children or our friends we sometimes become frustrated or annoyed because they just don't "get it "—whatever "it" may be. The truth is, in many cases, they just haven't experienced this event or circumstances in the same way we have! Perhaps they haven't experienced this event or circumstance at all! A great deal of patience, understanding and enlightenment are required to understand why people do or say what they do.

I believe that one of the best ways (though perhaps not the quickest) to find your inner bliss is to learn to completely and utterly accept people for who they are and not try to change them.

It will take work. With a healthy dose of self-confidence, you must strive for alignment, balance and clarity, but it can be done. Honestly, it is actually a lot more difficult than you may think. Almost all of us can be set in our ways at times, have difficulty with change or uncertainty and well, want to sometimes persuade others to our camps.

Surrendering is never complete without acceptance. You do not have to be in full agreement with acceptance of a certain situation or life circumstance. However, acceptance is powerful. The Dali Lama, the Pope and other spiritual leaders will confirm that acceptance is important not only to your peace and harmony, but that of our world as well.

Acceptance comes more easily to some than others. If you tend to have a controlling personality, surrender and acceptance will be uncomfortable for you.

Acceptance and surrender are very powerful. They have the power to bring great benefits to your life.

Remember, you are NOT giving up. You are NOT being defeated. You are permitting and letting go of an outcome for now. You are releasing the negativity and focusing only on the positive in this moment.

You can still be in control but in a healthier way. You are going to let all things flow naturally and effortlessly.

If acceptance and surrender are difficult for you, consider going to personal enrichment seminars, read books, or attend webinars to become more spiritually enlightened.

Chapter Twenty-Six
Urban Goddess Final Thoughts

"Follow your bliss and the universe will open doors where there were only walls." ~ Joseph Campbell

Some of my clients love their stronger self-confidence and inner bliss. Transformation brings a higher level of self-motivation, inspiration and inner harmony.

Some of my clients, after implementing some of the work we did together, do well for a period of time but then take a backward step. This is normal and natural, especially for those who are skeptical of a new way of thinking and behaving.

Throughout this book, my goal has been to give you the emotional tools, thoughts and inspiration that have worked with many, many people to enhance and better themselves.

Perhaps you owe it to yourself (and to those you love and who love you) that if you feel you are missing something in your life, if you are aching for that something more, that you take a chance and search for the answers you seek.

Drastic changes do sometimes happen, but the most significant changes in our lives usually take place slowly and gradually, one small change building upon another until transformation occurs.

Throughout the book I have asked you to ask yourself one of the most important questions you can ever answer: How is this working for me?

If there is something off, something missing, something stirring inside of your soul, don't bury your head in the sand. Don't just rationalize it or push it away. Acknowledge it. Find out what it is. It could be your key to sublime happiness if you find the answer but you will never know until you try!

We usually don't realize how precious time really is and what a gift our life is until:

- ✎ We experience a great deal of loss in our lives, OR

- ✎ We are told that our time here may be more limited than we had anticipated.

Yes, there is one more caveat I would like to add. That is a different type of loss but a loss nonetheless. It is the loss of never knowing who you were born to be.

If you continue to be yourself throughout the course of your life — truly authentic and transparent — it is only then that you shall have the answers to who you are and what your passions are.

Being mindful and respectful, and nurturing your sense of self will help to transform you into a whole person. You will never need another "half" ever, but you may very well want another whole person. Look for one that can walk the walk with you on your journey.

Being all you can be throughout your life and knowing how to do that effortlessly will make your life much less stressful. Best of all, no matter where you live, whether it is in a big, crowded city or a quiet rural area, your energy will radiate and your mind and spirit will know when to tap into your peace.

Being all you can be is a gift that you give yourself by honoring yourself. No one else can bring you that gift.

You will experience fewer days of uncertainty or frustration. Fewer days of confusion or sadness. Yes, life will still "happen" but now you also know that you can be the mistress of your own thoughts and take charge of your reaction to any given situation.

When you choose, choose love. Choose respect. Choose harmony. Choose what's right for you. You will be rewarded by other like-minded people and energies coming your way. You will naturally manifest them to you.

Nothing is ever set in stone. The world is an evolving, changing place filled with billions of souls and energies. Be true to you. Have no regrets.

Bask in the glow of living a life as an Urban Goddess.

Inspirational Quotes

"Never be bullied into silence. Never allow yourself to be made a victim. Accept no one's definition of your life, but define yourself."
— Harvey Fierstein

"Happiness is like a butterfly; the more you chase it the more it will elude you but if you turn your attention to other things, it will come and sit softly on your shoulder." — Thoreau

"The worst loneliness is not be comfortable with yourself." — Mark Twain

"You are always with yourself so you might as well enjoy the company."
— Diane Von Furstenberg

"Do one thing every day that scares you." — Eleanor Roosevelt

"Crying is for plain women, pretty women go shopping." — Oscar Wilde

"A great figure of physique is nice, but it's self confidence that makes someone really sexy." — Vivica Fox

"And when you want something all the universe conspires in helping you achieve it." — Paul Coelho

"It can be done, but you have to make it happen." — Chris Gardner

"If you live to be 100, I hope I live to be 100 minus one day so I never have to live without you." — from Winnie the Pooh

Recommended Readings

Amara, Heather Ash. *Warrior Goddess Training: Become the Woman You Are Meant to Be.* The antidote to the flawed idea that you are not enough. Drawing on the wisdom from Buddhism, Toltec wisdom, and ancient Earth-based goddess spirituality, the Warrior Goddess path includes personal stories, rituals, and exercises that will encourage and inspire you to become the true warrior goddess you are meant to be.

Bancroft, Lundy. *Why Does He Do That? Inside the Minds of Angry and Controlling Men.* A veteran of work with abusive men, Bancroft covers early warning signs, ten abusive personality types, the abusive mentality, problems with getting help from the legal system, and the long, complex process of change.

Brown, Sandra. *How to Spot a Dangerous Man Before You Get Involved.* This savvy, straightforward book pairs real women's stories with research and the expertise of a domestic violence counselor to help women of all ages identify Dangerous Men – before they become too involved.

Carpineto, Jane. *The Don Juan Dilemma: Should Women Stay with Men Who Stray.* A psychotherapist examines the compulsive behavior known as womanizing.

Chapman, Gary D. *The Five Love Languages: The Secret to Love that Lasts.* Dr. Gary Chapman's proven approach to showing and receiving love to help couples experience deeper and richer levels of intimacy.

Dalai Lama. *Healing Anger: The Power of Patience from a Buddhist Perspective.* In this book, the Dalai Lama shows how through the practice of patience and tolerance we can overcome the obstacles of anger and hatred.

de Becker, Gavin. *The Gift of Fear and Other Survival Signals that Protect Us from Violence.* The man Oprah Winfrey calls the nation's leading expert on violent behavior shows you how to spot even subtle signs of danger before it's too late.

Engel, Beverly. *Loving Him without Losing You: How to Stop Disappearing and Start Being Yourself.* Examines the intricate reasons why so many women submerge themselves in their relationships with men.

Golomb, Elan. *Trapped in the Mirror: Adult Children of Narcissists in Their Struggle for Self.* Golomb identifies the crux of the emotional and psychological problems of millions of adults—offspring of parents whose interest always towered above the most basic needs of their sons and daughters—share a common belief: They believe they do not have the right to exist.

Horley, Sandra. *Power and Control: Why Charming Men Can Make Dangerous Lovers.* The author draws on over twenty years supporting abused women to provide an insight into the reality behind the mask of the charming man.

La Roche, Loretta. *Life is Short, Wear Your Party Pants.* A book of tools you need to not only reduce feelings of tension, but also to bring joy, passion, and gusto into your life.

Lowen, Alexander. *Narcissism: Denial of the True Self.* Dr. Alexander Lowen uses his extensive clinical experience to demonstrate how narcissists can recover their suppressed feelings and regain their lost humanity.

McBride, Karyl. *Will I Ever Be Good Enough?: Healing the Daughters of Narcissistic Mothers.* A book specifically for daughters suffering from the emotional abuse of selfish, self-involved mothers.

Meyer, Joyce. *Enjoying Where You Are on the Way to Where You Are Going: Learning How to Live a Joyful Spirit-Led Life.* Joyce Meyer combines biblical principles with personal experiences for a powerful teaching on how to enjoy every day on your journey through life.

Miller, Alice. *The Drama of the Gifted Child: The Search for the True Self.* A profound book about childhood trauma that provides readers with guidance and hope.

Nelson, Noelle. *Dangerous Relationships: How to Identify and Respond to the Seven Warning Signs of a Troubled Relationship.* Nelson highlights dangerous turning points in relationships and explains how readers can safely diffuse tension between their spouses, lovers, or roommate and protect themselves from abuse.

Orloff, Judith. *The Ecstasy of Surrender: 12 Surprising Ways Letting Go Can Empower Your Life.* Dr. Judith Orloff proposes the art of letting go is the secret key to manifesting power and success in all areas of life, including work, relationships, sexuality, radiant aging, and health and healing.

Robbins, Anthony. *Awaken the Giant Within: How to Take Immediate Control of Your Mental, Emotional, Physical and Financial Destiny.* Anthony Robbins, the nation's leader in the science of peak performance, shows you his most effective strategies and techniques for mastering your emotions, your body, your relationships, your finances, and your life.

Schaffer, Brenda. *Is It Love or Is It Addiction: The Book That Changed the Way We Think About Romance and Intimacy.* A licensed psychologist and certified addiction specialist writes on love addiction: what it is and what it is not, how to identify it, and, even more important, how to break free of it.

Simon, George. *Character Disturbance: The Phenomenon of our Age.* Addresses how modern permissiveness and the new culture of entitlement allow disturbed people to reach adulthood without proper socialization.

Simon, George. *In Sheep's Clothing: Understanding and Dealing with Manipulative People.* A guide for understanding the tactics of manipulative people and how to deal with them.

Somp, Caroline. *A Year of Little Things: 100 Simple Ways to be Happy.* A gentle guide to making every moment count, inviting you to slow down and embrace the simple pleasures of daily life.

Zukav, Gary. *The Seat of the Soul.* Using his scientist's eye and philosopher's heart, Zukav shows how infusing the activities of life with reverence, compassion, and trust makes them come alive with meaning and purpose.

About the Author

Laney (Elaine) Zukerman is a certified life coach, professional counselor, author and mom.

A native New Yorker, she grew up in Brooklyn. Before her move to New York City, she raised her daughters Jaclyn and Laura in Westchester County, New York. Today, Laney works as a personal counselor and educator at a college in New York City and also operates a private practice specializing in relationship issues, empowerment and lifestyle coaching.

Prior to her coaching and counseling career, she worked for over a decade as a celebrity manager and public relations consultant to a number of national charities, including the March of Dimes and the American Cancer Society. And, tapping into her experience as a former cable television producer, she currently helps to mom-manage both her daughters' media and modeling careers.

Laney enjoys living the ultimate Urban Goddess lifestyle and has found her passion in helping empower and encourage women from all walks of life to live their best lives.

Lessons for an Urban Goddess is also available as an e-book.

You can contact Laney at laney@laneyzukerman.com

Visit Laney's website at laneyzukerman.com

www.ingramcontent.com/pod-product-compliance
Lightning Source LLC
Chambersburg PA
CBHW061146040426
42445CB00013B/1581